THE MYTHICAL STATE
OF
JEFFERSON

A PICTORIAL HISTORY
OF EARLY
NORTHERN CALIFORNIA
AND
SOUTHERN OREGON

BY
JACK SUTTON

THE GREAT SEAL OF
STATE OF JEFFERSON
XX

Josephine County Historical Society

512 SW 5th Street

Grants Pass, OR 97526

(541) 479-7827

www.jocohistorical.org

First Printing

1965

Second Printing

2003

Third Printing

2013

ISBN-13: 978-1491071489

ISBN-10: 1491071486

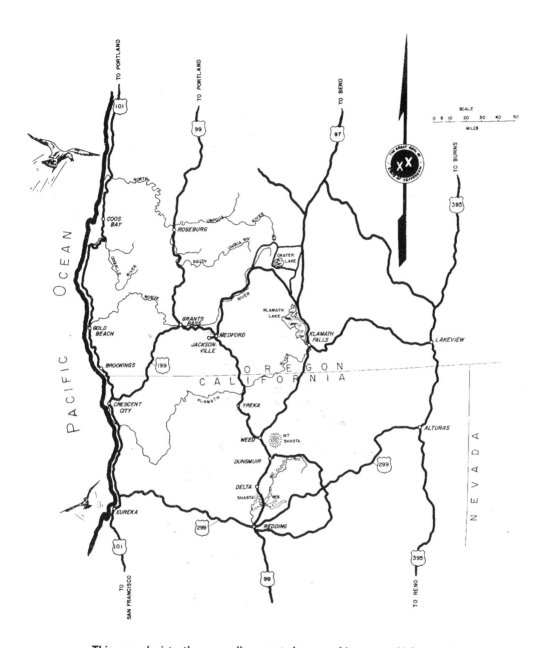

This map depicts the generally accepted geographic areas which comprise the mythical "State of Jefferson." No one is actually certain where the exact boundaries of the State are located, though it is generally agreed that they stretch from the Pacific Ocean to the high plateau beyond the Cascade and Sierra Nevada mountain ranges on the east, and between the 40th and 44th parallels. It is, however, unanimously agreed, that within Jefferson's natural borders lies a land of unbelievably rich undeveloped resourses, spectacular beauty, and an excitingly vivid past.

Table of Contents

Preface
The "State of Jefferson"

Few states of our Union can lay claim to the distinction of having flown as many flags as the mythical "State of Jefferson". Over this prolific soil have waved the banners of Spain, England, Russia, Mexico, the Bear Flag Republic and the United States of America.

Though more than two decades have elapsed since the official formation of the "State of Jefferson," this book may stir nostalgic sentiment among those readers who participated in the "revolt" leading to the secession movement of November, 1941.

Many motorists will recall that national attention was drawn to the new State with the setting up of road blocks on U.S. Highway 99 by Yreka residents to interrogate travelers crossing the Jefferson State "Line".

For the benefit of those skeptics who doubt that authoritative recognition of the State of Jefferson was ever granted beyond the realm of the local scene, we offer the following excerpts from Volume 31 of Marquis' "Who's Who in America:"

"Stanton Delaplane of the San Francisco Chronicle — received the Pulitzer prize (1941) for regional reporting of the movement of California and Oregon border counties to secede and form the 49th State."

This publication will trace earlier attempts at statehood to show the mythical State of Jefferson was but one in a long series of efforts in the complex field of separate-state agitation.

It has long been the common practice of textbook writers to record the early development of this region as history occurring in separate states, but the events themselves are so interwoven as to actually be inseparable when presenting the true chronicle.

Neither Indian nor early gold seeker bothered to determine the actual location of the border between the two states. Close elections were completely confused when the miners of Jacksonville, Waldo, (Sailor Diggin's) and other Southern Oregon gold producing centers voted in both states, but refused to pay taxes in either. Whenever a tax representative of the Oregon Territory called, he would find that the miners had just decided they were Californians. These same stalwarts would become staunch Oregonians by the time the California collector arrived on the scene. Yreka and Happy Camp also moved in this convenient pattern. It was not until the mid 1850's that the inhabitants finally became reconciled to the exact legal boundary.

Though the 20th Century movements have been largely tongue-in-cheek affairs, the mid-1800 efforts were "dead serious". The modern "rebellions" have been primarily perpetrated to achieve recognition by the respective state governments which have sometimes proven to be too remote from Jefferson's people to recognize their problems.

When the final gleaming rail of the Oregon California Railroad was laid in 1887, citizens of Jefferson believed that the isolation from the centers of commerce and culture in the states to which they had been committed would end with this transportation link. Further passage of time, however, dispelled this hope, and by the late 1930's the inherent rebel spirit of these people was thoroughly aroused. That the area's natural blessings and beauty were exploited by their respective states without thought of replentishment for future generations of Jeffersonians was too much to accept passively. Using the sad condition of existing roads and highways as their theme-song, the bordering counties of Oregon and California united in a determined effort to do something about the situation.

Judge John L. Childs of Crescent City was among those to spearhead the action, and the "State of Jefferson" was on its way.

Though the birth of the 1941 insurrection was at Gold Beach of Curry County, Oregon, this sport fishing center lost its bid for Jefferson's first gubernatorial district with the appointment of Judge Childs of Crescent City as the first "Governor."

The new plan took its first steps in the harbor city but it was the colorful showmanship of the Yreka citizenry led by J. P. Maginnis that put real spring in its stride.

Historians have recorded the momentous occasion that ushered in the Jeffersonian period as having begun with the Siskiyou Daily of November 3, 1941, banner headline reading: "Siskiyou Has Been Doublecrossed Again!" It could only follow that the state insignia evolving from this bold statement would bear the double-cross (XX) emblem as the official seal of the State of Jefferson.

On December 4, 1941, the Yreka Courthouse lawn was filled with advocates of the "Statehood" movement to inaugurate Judge Childs as acting Governor of Jefferson.

The occasion was crowned by the ringing speech of acceptance by the newly installed magistrate, as he recalled settling in Crescent City 50 years before, when there was no passable road into Klamath River country. His stirring remarks dryly concluded with the fact that "there still wasn't!"

In Yreka's Siskiyou County Museum visitors may view the original gold pan which bears Jefferson's official State Seal (left-below).

Some of the motorists who were able to squeeze through the inauguration torchlight parade may have saved the handbills and "49th State" windshield stickers (right-below) given them at the "border-patrol" stations during the 1941 "rebellion." These were headed: "Proclamation of Independence," and listed some of the reasons for secession:

"You are now entering Jefferson, the 49th state of the Union. This state has seceded from California and Oregon this Thursday, November 27th, 1941. Patriotic Jeffersonians intend to secede each Thursday until further notice. For the next 100 miles as you drive along Highway 99, you are traveling parallel to the greatest copper belt in the far west, 70 miles west of here. The United States government needs this vital mineral but gross neglect by California and Oregon deprives us of the necessary roads to bring out the copper ore. If you don't believe this, drive down the Klamath River highway and see for yourself. Take your chains, shovel and dynamite.

"Until California and Oregon build a road into the copper country, Jefferson, as a defense minded state, will be forced to rebel each Thursday and act as a separate State.

The events of the inauguration, the parades, and the other carefully staged programs were recorded by newsreel companies and prepared for a December 8th, 1941, release date to theaters throughout the world.

One cannot help but wonder just how far the statehood effort might have been pursued had the Nation's attention not been diverted by the earth-shaking event at Pearl Harbor on December 7, 1941.   Jack Sutton—1965

★★★★★★★★★★★★
49
I Have Visited
Jefferson
The 49th State
YREKA
★★★★★★★★★★★★

Part 1
The Prehistoric Beginning

The recorded history of our mythical State of Jefferson dates back to the mid 16th century when Conquistadors and explorers sought riches and glory for the Spanish throne.

To find the story of the past before man's eye first viewed this area, we must examine the findings of the archaeologist, Thomas Condon, author of a text entitled "Two Islands."

In the distant ages when America was very young, the land which was to form the Pacific Northwest lay restless beneath the Pacific Ocean. Rising above the surface were at least two islands (above). The southernmost was to become the Siskiyou mountain range of Northern California and Southern Oregon (left-below).

Life came to these areas from the water, some by air and still other by land as the gap between the mainland of America and the island was closed by mountain chains rising from the ancient sea bed.

In this age of humid climate, many geologic eras before the appearance of the first mammals, lived the lizard-like reptiles (right-below). These were from amphibious sea life which had hatched eggs on the new island.

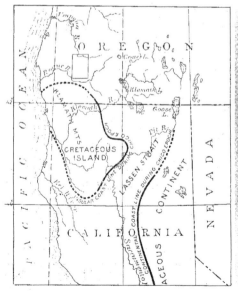

During a later period, the ancestor of today's camel and the Peruvian Llama (left-above), roamed our area with the three toed horse (right-above). This latter animal, originally no larger than a modern goat, had become extinct long before the Spanish brought the European horse to the American continent. Bones of both the early camel and three toed horse have been found in the ancient campsites of Southern Oregon's first human inhabitants.

Reminders of this prehistoric life continue to be brought to light by modern construction crews. Among the specimens displayed in Jefferson's museums are tusks and teeth from ancient mammoths (left-below), the ancestor of present day elephants (right-below).

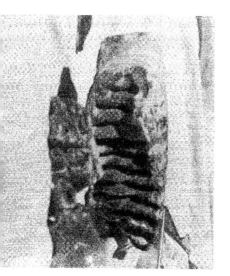 

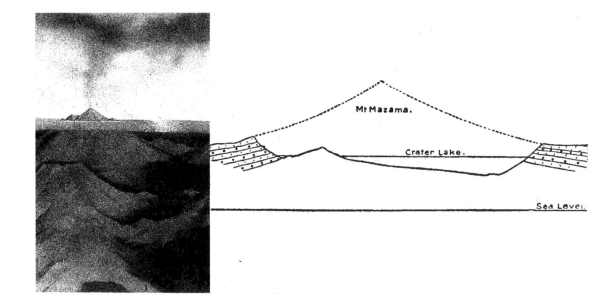

Mt Mazama.

Crater Lake.

Sea Level.

As the ancient sea bed continued to crumple and shift, a great sea dike of volcanic mountains began to rise between and beyond the two islands (left-above).

Vast inland seas were landlocked between this new land mass and the former shoreline of the North American mainland.

South of the Oregon-California border this mountain range is called the Sierra Nevadas. North of this boundary it is known as the Cascades.

Throughout the Ice Age, several giant peaks towered above this dike. One of these we have named Mt. Mazama. Rising to a height of more than 12,000 feet (right-above), it collapsed into its own crater (left-below), shutting off all volcanic action except for three gas escape cones. Natural water springs and rainfall filled the former crater to produce our present majestic Crater Lake. One of the small cones within the crater remains today as Wizard Island (right-below).

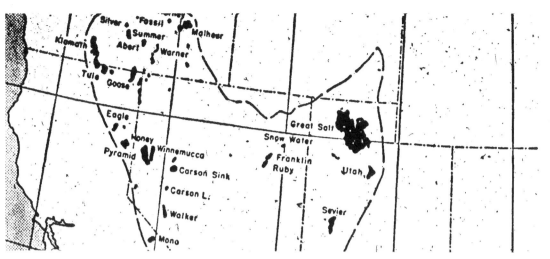

To further landlock the old sea, another barrier we call the Coast mountains arose. The inland seas worked their way through the mountain blockades to create drainage outlets such as the mighty Columbia, Rogue, Klamath, Sacramento and other major rivers. The pattern of today's geography was completed with the formation of hundreds of lesser streams draining the Pacific slope.

After long centuries of evaporation and drainage, only the Great Salt Lake and a few lesser bodies of water remain to remind us of the landlocked sea (above).

Near the close of the Ice Age and with the beginning of Jefferson's climate as we know it, came the first inhabitants of whom we are presently aware. The principal known route of these people from their native Asia was by way of the Bering Strait (left-below).

Though often regarded by the white man as a single family, the many tribes within Jefferson's boundaries (right-below) differed widely in culture, custom and language.

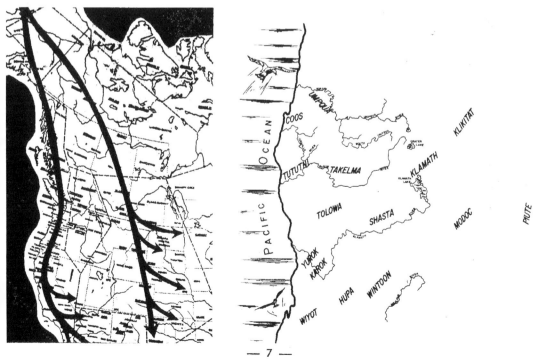

A complete story of our early Indian tribes and their customs would easily fill this volume. Within the brief space allotted the general history of our region we can discuss their way of life only in broad terms.

The physical appearance of Jefferson's Indians was similiar to those of midwestern America. Slightly shorter in stature than the white population of the same era, both sexes were usually well proportioned. Their brown skin color ranged from a light yellow to dark reddish tone.

Through the summer months, clothing presented little problem since little, if any, was worn. During the cooler periods of the year the most common garments used were made from dressed deer skins and shredded tree bark (left-above).

Living quarters varied widely to include portable shelters of skins and reeds (center-above); wickiups of tree limb framework, covered with mud or sod (right-above); and more elaborately constructed houses of split planks (left-below). These homes often served more than a single family.

Some of the Northern California Shastas lived in the numerous natural caves of the Klamath River region (right-below).

In the summer months, most tribes set up temporary huts beside their favored fishing creeks or rivers.

Ceremonies and dances played an important role in Indian community life. One colorful ten day ritual, called the "white deerskin dance", included a display of albino deer skins carried on long ceremonial poles (left-above).

Of the many varieties of headresses worn on these occasions, among the most highly prized was one decorated with rows of redheaded woodpecker scalps sewn to a buckskin base (right-above).

Personal grooming for ceremonies included the painting of both male and female faces. No fixed patterns were followed though three horizontal stripes were most common (left-below).

Woodpecker scalps were also used as money, but the most common article employed for this purpose was the hiaqua shell called dentalium. Purses carved from an elk antler were sometimes used to protect dentalium strings from being crushed (right-below).

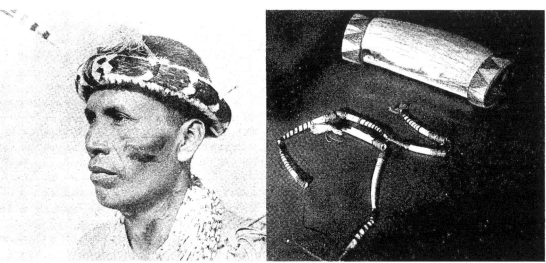

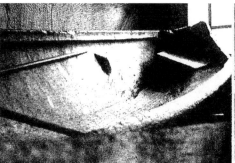

The scow type canoe was used for fishing, gathering of reeds for basket making (left and center-above) or travels to trade. Canoes were also used as a medium of exchange.

Weapons of the early tribes included the spear; obsidian or other rock knives; clubs of root, wood or rock, and the bow and arrow (left-below).

When preparing to do battle, the Yuroks of Northern California wore reed armor over a heavy elk skin war dress (right-above). Holding a supply of arrows in the mouth and still more under the arm, many of Jefferson's Indians were so expert in the use of the bow that they could release one arrow and have a second in flight before the first reached its mark.

The duty of providing meat for the Indian family was the man's task. A deerskin disguise with a set of mounted horns on a buckskin cap (center-below) was used to approach a herd to within effective bow range. This was about fifty yards.

Fishing with the forked end harpoon was also a highly developed male skill (right-below).

Harvesting and preparation of nature's foods such as berries, fruit, nuts and roots were among those chores handled by women.

The most common flour used for bread, puddings or soup was from the oak acorn gathered and prepared by the women of the tribe as a community enterprise (left-above). The acorns were ground on flat rocks or with mortar and pestle. The flour was then brushed from the tools with a small fiber broom (right-above).

One of the principal food sources among the Klamaths and Modocs was the pond lily. The hard shell of the pod was broken by pounding with lava rock (left-below).

Using the fire drill to provide flame for heating or cooking was the responsibility of the family head (center-below).

Cooking was accomplished in open fire broiling or with closely woven water tight baskets. To boil soups or other liquids a heated rock was picked up with a split or forked stick, the ashes blown off, and the rock dropped into the cooking basket (right-below). As the rocks cooled, they were removed and replaced with hot ones throughout the cooking process.

The elderly of Jefferson's tribes aided in many village chores including food preparation and the gathering of firewood (left-above). One of their principal duties was to serve as teachers for the children.

Sweat houses were used in the belief that induced perspiration could prevent or cure disease (right-above). The ritual concluded with a plunge into the river (left-below).

Men smoked a single pipeful of native "tobacco" each night. Stone or wooden pipes which could be smoked best lying down were used. (center-below).

Unlike many tribes to the north and east of Jefferson's boundaries, the "medicine man" was often a woman who used her pipe to eliminate the evil spirits of illnesses (right-below). In providing medicinal needs, the shaman had to select his or her cases with care since the relatives of those lost while under paid-for treatment could insist on the shaman being buried with his mistake.

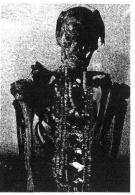

No written language was ever developed by these people, though many pictures were carved on clay or rocks to tell stories, convey warnings or portray routes of travel (left-above).

Most of Jefferson's tribes had been removed to reservations before the end of the Civil War. As a result, the Indian graves found by those seeking artifacts in the region today are more than a century old (center-above).

The bodies of those killed in battle were often cremated, while those who left the world in a less spectacular manner were buried in graveyards adjacent to their villages. The body, with articles of personal wealth, was buried in a sitting position with the arms lashed around the folded legs. Dentalium shell money was broken and placed in the mouth of the deceased. Eyes and ears were sometimes covered with sea shells (right-above).

For today's students of Indian lore, a number of fine artifact collections can be found in Jefferson's museums. Among the outstanding of these is the display at Fort Jones, California (left-below).

No one knows when the first outer world races were seen by these tribes, but it is most likely the first contact was with shipwrecked sailors and Chinese traders seeking furs.

Pieces of candlestick beeswax, originally consigned to the Spanish California missions, have provided positive evidence of early wrecks along Oregon's rugged shore. (right-below).

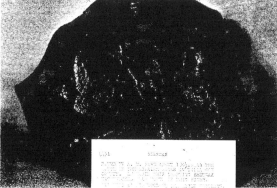

For nearly 200 years, the ships of many nations probed Jefferson's bays and inlets in a futile search for the mythical "Strait of Anian." The early navigators had sought this imaginary all-water passage through the heart of the American continent in the vain hope that they would find a more direct route between Europe and the wealth of the East Indies.

The first Spaniard to examine Jefferson's coast was Juan Rodrigues Cabrillo who sailed to the latitude of 44 degrees in 1542. He landed near Port Orford.

With the generous price on his head eagerly sought by fleets of Spanish men-of-war, Francis Drake turned his loot-laden "Golden Hynde" north in 1579 to search Jefferson's shores for this legendary "Northwest Passage."

Failing to find such a passage by the time he had sailed as far north as the Winchester Bay region of present Oregon, he returned south to San Francisco Bay to beach and repair his ship. Here he completed the work of readying his crew and gathering supplies needed to follow the wake of Magellan's "Victoria" across the Pacific, returning to England by way of the Cape of Good Hope.

Before leaving the bay, Drake claimed for his Queen that area we now call Jefferson, staking his claim by erecting an inscribed "plate of brass". This same plate now rests encased in glass at the Bancroft Library of the University of California at Berkeley (above).

It has only been in recent years that the beaching point was established as having been within San Francisco Bay. The plate was found near an outcropping rock formation described by Drake's own nephew (left-below).

The friendly Jefferson natives who crowned Drake "King" of the territory he named "New Albion", were not to remain so peaceful during the three centuries that followed this event. These Indians were among the last of the tribesmen to feel the pressure of the white man's conquest of North America.

Many historians have recorded the fierce savagery of Jefferson's Indian population. The twentieth century observer must remember, however, that the unfair dealings of the white man had become almost common knowledge among these tribes long before the gold rush years. Incidents recorded by early writers as "unprovoked" attacks or massacres were in truth the first steps toward a final stand against the inevitable and frequently ruthless intrusion of the White.

Aguila, a lieutenant of Sebastian Viscaino, named Cape Blanco on their expedition, which made the first known investigation of the Umpqua River in 1603 (right-below).

Spanish, English and American explorers continued to sail past Jefferson's shores with little more than a superficial glance for the next two centuries.

In 1808, the Russians, in their sea otter hunting expeditions, examined California's Bodega Bay as a possible permanent headquarters site to expand their trapping operations beyond Sitka, Alaska.

By 1812, the Russians had decided against the Bodega Bay location and in June sent an expedition to build an outpost 13 miles northwest of the Russian River (above). They called the fort "Colony Ross". The name Ross is believed to have come from the Russian word "Rus".

Fort Ross, as it is now known, contained fifty-nine buildings enclosed by a 14 foot stockade. At the north and south corners were two story blockhouses (left-below). Here were mounted 14 cannon which can be seen today at Sutter's Fort in Sacramento, California. These cannon were ones abandoned by Napoleon in his retreat from Moscow.

The post buildings included the commandant's house, a Russian Orthodox Chapel (right-below), a jail, dairy, blacksmith shop, bakery, two warehouses and a bath house.

Most of the articles made at the fort, such as harnesses, saddles, leather belts and bags, tile, and barrels were sent north to the main Russian colony at Sitka.

It is of interest to note that title for the land on which the colony stood was purchased from the Indians for 3 blankets, 3 pairs of trousers, two axes, three hoes and some beads. This is the only transaction in California records where land was actually bought instead of the normal procedure of simply taking possession and driving the Indians off.

North of Jefferson's borders, fur seekers had established a thriving business by the turn of the 18th century. The fur industry had begun with Robert Gray's 1792 discovery of the Columbia River and Lewis and Clark's overland expedition 12 years later.

By 1811, the first permanent fur trading fort was established at Astoria, Oregon. When Fort' Astoria was sold to Britain's Northwest Company in 1812, it was renamed Fort George and expanded to nearly three times its original size (left).

For 11 years, the "Nor'westers" controlled the Columbia River fur trade, merging with the older and more powerful Hudson's Bay Company in 1823. At this time Dr. John McLoughlin was assigned as chief factor for all Hudson's Bay outposts in the Oregon Country.

During 1824, the supply of coastal tribe furs dropped to an unprofitable low and McLoughlin built Fort Vancouver on the site of present Vancouver, Washington (below). This new post provided a more central operating base for trade brigades working the Willamette and upper Columbia rivers.

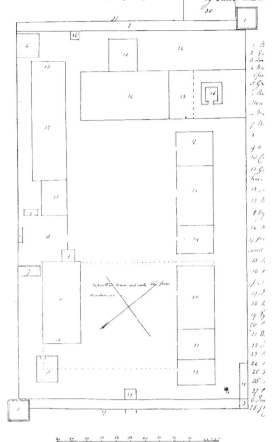

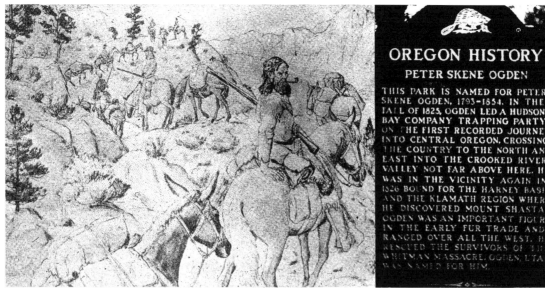

OREGON HISTORY

PETER SKENE OGDEN

THIS PARK IS NAMED FOR PETER SKENE OGDEN, 1793-1854. IN THE FALL OF 1825, OGDEN LED A HUDSON'S BAY COMPANY TRAPPING PARTY ON THE FIRST RECORDED JOURNEY INTO CENTRAL OREGON. CROSSING THE COUNTRY TO THE NORTH AND EAST INTO THE CROOKED RIVER VALLEY NOT FAR ABOVE HERE. HE WAS IN THE VICINITY AGAIN IN 1826 BOUND FOR THE HARNEY BASIN AND THE KLAMATH REGION WHERE HE DISCOVERED MOUNT SHASTA. OGDEN WAS AN IMPORTANT FIGURE IN THE EARLY FUR TRADE AND RANGED OVER ALL THE WEST. HE RESCUED THE SURVIVORS OF THE WHITMAN MASSACRE. OGDEN, UTAH WAS NAMED FOR HIM.

Between the years of 1825 and 1843, fifteen groups of trappers explored Jefferson in search of furs (left-above). The first official mention of the region would seem to be the Hudson's Bay records of 1814 in which Mount Shasta was described to the traders by Willamette valley Indians of Shasta tribe ancestry or marriage ties.

In 1825, a Hudson's Bay fur brigade under the command of Thomas McKay and Finan McDonald followed the Indian trails through the Willamette and Umpqua valleys, crossing the Rogue River a few miles west of present Grants Pass, Oregon; over the Siskiyou Mountains to the Scott Valley, and continued as far south as the McCloud and Sacramento rivers of California.

This same year, Peter Skene Ogden, assistant to Dr. McLoughlin, began an expedition to determine possible trading station locations along the eastern slopes of the Cascades (right-above).

Ogden arrived at Upper Klamath Lake in December, 1826 (left-below). Based upon favorable reports of these early expeditions, an outpost was established a few miles south of present Yreka, California.

In the Siskiyou County Museum are displays of trade items and Hudson's Bay articles dug from the old post site. Near this location was the earliest dated tombstone (1834) ever found within Jefferson's boundaries (right-below).

Jedediah Smith and 17 other American trappers comprised the first party to travel north through Jefferson's vast expanse. In 1828, this group decided to avoid the danger of Indian raids on the southern trail to St. Louis by working their way north to Fort Vancouver. From this point they planned to follow the old mountain men's trail to the east.

To miss the tortuous trails over the Siskiyou Mountains, they turned west to the coast from the Sacramento Valley and made their way north to the Umpqua River.

The party camped on the north bank of the Smith River channel near present Reedsport. Following an argument over a stolen axe, Indians killed all but one of the men in camp (right-above). Smith and two companions were looking for a river crossing when the attack took place.

Ten days after the massacre, the sole survivor reached Fort Vancouver and was soon joined by Smith and John Turner. The latter pair had been guided to the fort by friendly Tillamooks.

Dr. McLoughlin sent Thomas McKay, his field captain, with Alexander Roderick McLeod's company of 49 men to recover the Smith party's furs.

Within two weeks, the Hudson's Bay men returned with most of the pelts. McLoughlin purchased these at the fair market value after deducting the cost of their recovery as based on McLeod's records (right-center and below).

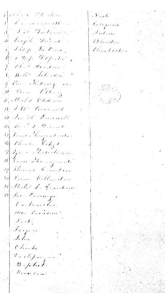

The next year, a trapping expedition, under McLeod, retraced the route travelled by Smith (above). Following the coast to the Klamath River, McLeod turned inland to the Sacramento valley. In a severe snowstorm he lost many of his pack horses and was forced to cache the furs collected near present Mc-Cloud, California.

McLeod returned to Vancouver by way of the Rogue and Umpqua valleys. A party sent out in 1830 to recover the furs found them spoiled by the severe winter.

In 1832, the Hudson's Bay men established the first Fort Umpqua on a plain of 200 acres near Elkton, Oregon, to trade with local and coastal tribes for beaver and seal pelts. The fort included log huts, a barn and a storehouse. It was enclosed by a 12 foot high log stockade with bastians at two of the corners.

Jason Lee, whose Methodist mission near Salem was the first in the Oregon country (left-below), used Fort Umpqua as his base of operations while preaching to the Umpqua tribes (right-below). His was the only attempt made to convert Jefferson's natives until the establishment of reservations in the mid 1850's.

Part IV
Jefferson's First Tourists

A school teacher, Hall Jackson Kelley, visited Oregon in 1834. His route followed the Indian and Hudson's Bay trails through Jefferson's Sacramento, Rogue and Umpqua valleys. He was accompanied by an old trapper and former mountain man, Ewing Young. Mistaking the Kelley and Young party for a group of California horse thieves, Dr. McLoughlin's reception was so cold that Kelley wrote bitter articles denouncing British treatment of Americans. His writings forced President Andrew Jackson to send Lt. William Slacum of the U.S. Navy to investigate the actual conditions.

Slacum discovered that one of the principal problems of the American settlers in the Oregon country concerned the lack of food producing domestic animals. Slacum, with McLoughlins aid, helped to organize a plan for purchasing California mission cattle. Ewing Young was chosen as leader of the venture and the group taken to Yerba Buena, later to become San Francisco (above), aboard Slacum's brig, the "Loriot".

Spanish colonial law forbade the export of cattle and permission for their purchase had to be obtained from Monterey. By accepting nearly wild cattle from the ranches adjoining the mission at San Jose, Young was able to assemble a larger herd than originally anticipated.

Making such a herd trail wise was difficult and the first sixty miles to the San Joaquin river took 30 days. At this crossing many cattle had to be towed across and 17 were drowned (left-below).

The drive followed the Indian trails through Jefferson's Siskiyou Mountains (right-below). Though the Shasta tribes kept a constant watch on Young's crew, they did not attempt to raid the herd.

At Foots Creek, near present Gold Hill, Oregon, an attack by the Takelma Indians was beaten off with the loss of one cow and the wounding of several others.

The weary drovers finally reached the Willamette valley in late 1836. They had made the trip with 630 of the original 800 head which had left San Jose nine months before.

In 1839, Johann August Sutter became one of the largest property owners in North America. Today, his restored fort in the heart of modern Sacramento, California, takes the visitor back to the period when Sutter's empire was at its peak (below).

Much of the material used in the fort came from the Russian Fort Ross which Sutter bought for $2,000 down.

The remaining balance of $28,000 was to have been paid to the Russian government in yearly installments of wheat and other produce.

Many of the buildings and equipment, 1,700 head of cattle, 940 horses and mules, and 9,000 sheep were transported to Sutter's domain on a 20 ton schooner also included in the trade.

Sutter hired Pierson B. Reading as a beaver trapper to work toward Jefferson's Oregon border. Reading's expeditions failed to produce enough good pelts to justify continuing the venture.

Deeply impressed with Jefferson's possibilities, Reading applied to the Mexican government for, and was granted, a claim of 20,000 acres north of Sutter's lands.

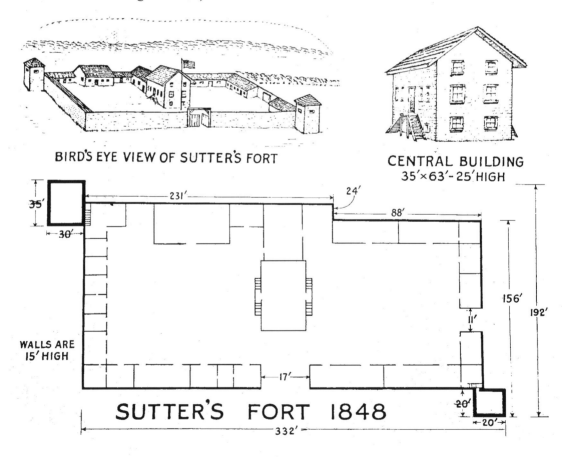

BIRD'S EYE VIEW OF SUTTER'S FORT

CENTRAL BUILDING
35'×63'-25' HIGH

SUTTER'S FORT 1848

WALLS ARE 15' HIGH

An extensive survey of the Oregon Country's river and harbors was made by Charles Wilkes for the U.S. Navy in 1841.

Wilkes detailed an expedition under Lt. Emmons to examine the Hudson's Bay trail from Fort Vancouver, through Jefferson and the Sacramento Valley, and rejoin the fleet at Yerba Buena (above).

In his report, Wilkes claimed the mouth of the Columbia River to be unsafe and that Puget Sound, north to latitude 54°40" (the southern Alaskan boundary) should be claimed by the United States to control the Northwest.

Though Wilkes conceded that the Bay of San Francisco had commercial possibilities, he erred slightly in his evaluation of Jefferson's fertile valleys with: "Only a small portion of the country offers any agricultural advantage . . . a large part of Sacramento valley is undoubtedly barren and must forever remain so."

Ewing Young's cattle venture had not completely relieved the Willamette valley's livestock shortage. A group of 6 farmers conceived the idea of building a boat which could be sailed to San Francisco Bay and traded for cattle. The keel was laid on the east side of Swan Island, Portland in May, 1840. The finished schooner was launched and christened the "Star of Oregon" in May of the following year (below).

Joseph Gale was the only member of the amateur shipbuilders ever to have been to sea. Wilkes, whose fleet was then anchored at Astoria, examined Gale for his ship's captain papers "by correspondence". Questions and answers were shuttled to and from Astoria and present Portland by riders on horseback.

Under Gale's command the schooner was sailed to San Francisco and traded for 350 cattle. Before returning to Oregon, the successful ship builders talked 42 Californians into moving to the Willamette valley. This total company and their livestock was many times larger than the earlier Ewing Young venture. In the spring of 1842 they followed the same route north taken by Young. Though a considerable number of livestock was driven off and stolen by the Shastas between the Klamath and Rogue rivers, Gale's crew and the new settlers made the journey without major incident.

The herd of bachelor Ewing Young had become quite large before his death in 1841. Since no heirs immediately claimed his property the need for a government to dispose of estates became a matter of dire need. With Young's cattle running wild and no organized means of protecting them, wolves and cougars became more bold in their attacks, endangering the entire Willamette valley stock.

In early 1843, "Wolf Meetings" were called to unite the settlers in establishing a wild animal bounty system. These settlers met at Champoeg, Oregon, and established a provisional government (left-below) which was to control the area south of the Columbia River, electing Joe Meek, one of the most famous of the early trappers, as their first sheriff.

With the proceeds from the settlement of Young's estate, the new government erected its first public building. This was the territorial jail at Oregon City (right-below).

The structure was just about escape-proof but it burned to the ground 14 months after completion. Governor Abernethy made an astute observation in his conclusion that it was "the work in his conclusion that it was "the work,

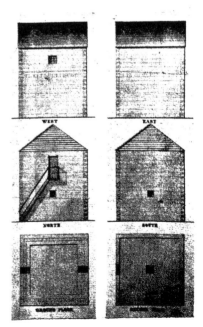

Several small bands of settlers had used the Oregon Trail prior to 1843. It was not until this year, however, that the great western migration began with a train of 875 settlers. The wagons assembled at the courthouse of Independence, Missouri, before beginning their westward trek (above).

This train brought many individuals who were destined to become famous in Jefferson's history. These included: California's first governor, Peter Burnett, the Applegate families, and James Nesmith.

Modern entertainment mediums seem to invariably depict the mode of travel vehicle as Conestoga covered wagons drawn by plodding oxen. In reality nearly every type of conveyance ever designed was pressed into service to reach the west in the pre-1850 years (left-below).

Most wagons were overloaded with prized family possessions, most of which would be discarded before the journey's end (right-below).

The last and often most hazardous leg of the journey required "boating" down the Columbia River from The Dalles to Fort Vancouver.

John C. Fremont and Kit Carson, leading an expedition sponsored by the United States, followed the route of Peter Skene Ogden east of the Cascades to the Klamath country. Their camp at Hot Creek was attacked by Modocs who thought that the killing of these whites would discourage further travel through their lands. In the fight, 3 of Fremont's Indian guides were killed.

The Fremont expedition continued south past present Reno and Carson City to Lake Tahoe through a severe winter storm which cost thirty-four horses and mules (left-above). Arriving at Sutter's in March of 1844, they were given a warm welcome. Among the reminders marking Kit Carson's visit is a carved tree trunk displayed at today's restored Fort Sutter (right-above).

In 1846 Fremont was again encamped in Oregon and moved from his base to capture the Spanish presido of Sonoma (below). This was the action which created the California Republic with its bear flag symbol.

Stephen Meek, brother of Oregon's first territorial sheriff, attempted to guide a wagon train by a route avoiding the difficult Blue Mountains and the dangerous river passage down the Columbia River. The alternate route he sought was to follow the Malheur River and cross central Oregon's Harney Basin. It is believed that he was trying to reach the Santiam Pass.

Meek had travelled this route as a Hudson's Bay trapper. In his effort to retrace the trail for the 1845 emigrants he became lost. The venture cost 20 lives before it was abandoned in favor of the old route. It was this party which found "yellow rocks" they hammered into fishing sinkers (below), never suspecting they had made the first Oregon gold discovery. Because of two blue buckets left at the scene, the story became the legend of the "Blue Bucket Mine".

Expansion of the territorial claims of the United States became a major issue of the 1844 Presidential campaign. The Democratic party, seeking to elect James Polk demanded American occupation of the entire Oregon country to the Alaskan border with the slogan of "54°-40" or fight".

To claim the entire area could force war with England and the fear of such a conflict led to a search for a new route to the Willamette valley. This new route would be one which could avoid British Fort Hall, and allow American troops and supplies to reach the Willamette valley.

A toll road over the south side of Mount Hood was opened in 1846 by Samuel Barlow (above). The Barlow road was limited to summer use due to the heavy winter snow pack, and a more satisfactory route to bypass British Fort Hall was still needed.

Leaving their brother, Charles, in charge of their family affairs, Jesse and Lindsay Applegate joined with Levi Scott and twelve others to examine Jefferson's Southern Oregon boundary. The explorations of Cornellius Gilliam had indicated a pass through the Cascade mountain range might be found in this region.

Jesse and Lindsay had each lost a son when their boats had overturned on the Columbia River and were anxious to help in the finding of a safer route.

Leaving Oregon City in June, 1846, the expedition travelled south through the present Oregon towns of Eugene, Roseburg, Grants Pass and Medford to the Klamath valley, fording Lost River at the Natural Bridge crossing near Humboldt, Nevada, by the present towns of Winnemucca, Elko and Wells, and joined with the Oregon Trail near Pocatello, Idaho (below).

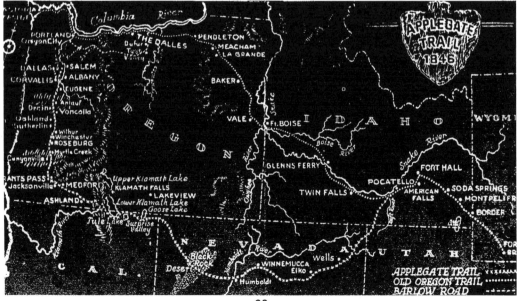

At Fort Hall, Jesse Applegate presented a glowing description of the new route and nearly 100 wagons decided to try the trail, leaving Fort Hall in early August, 1846 (right-above).

Near the Humbolt River, attacks from poisoned Indian arrows took their toll of both cattle and immigrants. Progress was slow due to steep hills which would often require all of the train's oxen to pull a single wagon to the summit. (right-center).

With disease, the barren desert, sharp rocks of the lava beds which quickly cut horse and oxen shoes to bits, added to the constant raids of the Pitt River, Klamath and Modoc Indians trying to steal cattle, the group became widely scattered on the trail and food supplies ran low or were completely exhausted.

Only the heroic efforts of the more hardy aiding the stricken (right-below) brought the survivors through to Jefferson's refreshing Rogue valley.

Before attempting the remaining barriers of the Umpqua and Calapooya mountains, the train made camp beside a mountain stream in Sunny Valley, Oregon. Here a fourteen year old girl named Martha Leland Crowley died and was buried beneath an oak tree (above-left). After filling the grave, horses and oxen were corraled about the tree to pack the earth and hide the location from the Indians.

Despite these precautions, the Indians however, found the grave, salvaged the clothing and placed the body in the limbs of the tree. The bones were found and reburied in 1848 by California bound prospectors. The name Grave Creek was given the area and still re-mains so despite efforts of later settlers to change it.

Today, the unmarked grave is near the south footing of the Grave Creek covered bridge (right-above).

Through November, 1846, the party fought its way down narrow Canyon Creek (left-below). Wagons were abandoned, those strong enough to ride mounted their animals (right-below). Many died of shock and exposure and the passage was littered with abandoned wagons and keepsakes. These were quickly claimed by the Umpqua Indians following the train, some of whom killed John Newton with the powder and shot he had given them.

Less than half of the party lived to reach the Willamette valley. This Southern Route or Applegate Trail was bitterly denounced by Governor George Abernathy in an 1847 circular letter (right-above).

Markers now outline the trail through Jefferson (left-below). This shorter route was to see far greater use during the gold rush years than the Oregon Trail knew through its entire history.

The same train to which the first Southern Route emigrants had belonged had been split once before. At Fort Bridger one section under George Donner attempted to follow an untried trail suggested in a book by Lansford Hastings (right-below).

After fighting through thicket choked canyons to present Reno the group started too late to miss the unusually severe winter. Because of the more than twenty foot deep snowdrifts, they were forced to make camp at Alder Creek and Donner Lake. Here, many of the survivors remained alive only by eating the flesh of the dead until help made its way from the Sacramento valley to rescue the 45 remaining of the original party of 81.

THE

EMIGRANTS' GUIDE,

TO

OREGON AND CALIFORNIA,

CONTAINING SCENES AND INCIDENTS OF A PARTY OF
OREGON EMIGRANTS;

A DESCRIPTION OF OREGON;

SCENES AND INCIDENTS OF A PARTY OF CALIFORNIA
EMIGRANTS;

AND

A DESCRIPTION OF CALIFORNIA;

A DESCRIPTION OF THE DIFFERENT ROUTES TO
THOSE COUNTRIES;

AND

ALL NECESSARY INFORMATION RELATIVE TO THE
EQUIPMENT, SUPPLIES, AND THE METHOD
OF TRAVELING.

BY LANSFORD W. HASTINGS,
Leader of the Oregon and California Emigrants of 1842.

CINCINNATI:
PUBLISHED BY GEORGE CONCLIN,
STEREOTYPED BY SHEPARD & CO.
1845.

The small community of Yerba Buena (above) had developed around the Mission of St. Francis of Assisi (left-below). The mission took its present name of Dolores from that of a nearby marsh. The first Mass of the mission was conducted five days before the Declaration of Independence.

The rapid growth of Yerba Buena was due in part to Sutter's expanded activities, which included the raising of wheat, flour milling, distilling of whiskey, a woolen mill and a passenger and freight boat service on the Sacramento River.

Sutter also began to erect his own warehouses at Yerba Buena. To provide lumber for this and his other enterprises, he built a water powered sawmill in the Coloma valley, about 18 hours ride from his fort (right-below).

To complete the mill construction, he hired 3 members of a caravan moving south from Oregon. Among these carpenters were James Marshall and Charles Bennett.

Water was turned into the millrace of the nearly completed sawmill to test and level the ditch on January 24, 1848. The washing action uncovered a gold nugget about ¼" in diameter, which was picked up by Marshall and Bennett and taken to Sutter (left-above).

Fearing what would happen to his empire, Sutter swore the men to secrecy, but the men at the mill began to examine and mine the adjoining area.

The "California Star" newspaper carried only a small column of the discovery because not too great interest was aroused (right-above) since gold had been previously found in small quantities in other parts of California.

About six years prior to the Coloma find, small quantities of gold had been found in Placerita Canyon near Los Angeles. Another early discovery dated back to 1824, when a pair of Mexican miners had worked Alamitos Creek near San Jose (below).

Sam Brannon, editor of the "California Star" went to investigate the rumor of the strike at Coloma. He returned with a whiskey flask filled with gold nuggets and the stampede was on. Every able bodied man in California, as well as many of the infirm, set out for the gold fields. By June, nearly every male citizen from Monterey, San Francisco, San Jose and Santa Cruz was in the vicinity of American River.

Part V
Years of the Golden Harvest

On August 1, 1848, the schooner "Honolulu" docked at Portland, Oregon. After the captain had quietly bought all the shovels and picks available in the two hardware stores, he announced the gold discovery news. Two thirds of the Oregon men joined the rush to California. Most of them traveled the old Hudson's Bay trail through Jefferson in organized caravans. One of the first of these groups was led by Peter Burnett who had hastily resigned his office as chief justice of Oregon.

Until this time, many of Jefferson's Indians had never imagined that so many whites even existed. The trails were easily followed because of Indian signal fires atop the bordering mountain ridges. These had been set by the Indians to alert their neighboring tribes.

Some Oregonians went by ship to Yerba Buena, now mushrooming into a huge tent city that was to become San Francisco (below).

As the natural shipping center for the gold fields, San Francisco grew from a population of 812 in January of 1848, to 40,000 within a single year.

The real surge westward from the eastern seaboard began when California's Governor Mason advised the War Department that California's "free" gold was sufficient "to pay the cost of the Mexican War a hundred times over".

Traffic on the wagon roads to California became so heavy that at one time westbound trains passed in an unbroken stream between Missouri and Fort Laramie for two months.

Though it was at first believed that only the Coloma valley was rich in gold, the precious metal was found in nearly every direction from Sutter's mill. In the summer of 1848, Pierson Reading struck gold near present Douglas City, California.

A short time after this discovery, a miner by the name of John Scott, found nuggets in quantities sufficient to draw hordes of miners to the Shasta River. The new "diggins" was called Scott's Bar (above).

Even the barrier of Jefferson's towering peaks failed to discourage the flood of rugged adventurers who eagerly sought her golden wealth, once the secret of hidden treasure was revealed. New trails were blazed through Jefferson as each day brought news of a new gold strike in the vast domain.

The new trails soon became the principal routes for delivery of needed supplies by packers and freighters. Whiskey, food and mail were delivered over these new "roads" through Jefferson's wilderness in the order listed. (below)

Arrival of mail was an eagerly awaited event since the miner who struck it rich was anxious to let those at home know his good fortune. The less successful seeker was just as anxious to gain sympathy or a "grubstake" to carry him until his fortune changed.

Uprisings of the Plains and Southwestern Indians made over-land mail delivery a hazardous (left-above) and expensive operation since military escorts were needed to prevent attacks (right-above).

Lone express riders were frequently the victims of Indian ambush (below).

It was decided that more direct and safe delivery of mail could be accomplished by water to a coastal point adjacent to Jefferson's inland mines. Secretary of the Navy, William Aspinwall, issued a directive calling for monthly delivery of mail "by sailing vessel, at or near the mouth of the Klamath River".

Two minor problems were posed by this excellent plan. One was the fact that no one had yet found the mouth of the Klamath River. The other was that most sailing vessels sent to the Pacific coast made only one way trips since the crews deserted as soon as the ships docked at San Francisco (above).

As this graveyard of ships began to mount, Yankee ingenuity came to the fore to convert many of the hulks into warehouses and business stores (below).

In 1850, a group of 35 men set sail from San Francisco in a leaky schooner named the "Samuel Roberts". Their goal was the mouth of the Klamath River specified in the Navy mail contract.

The party called itself "the Klamath Expedition" and planned to establish a town at the place scheduled for mail shipments. Such a town could control most of the traffic into Jefferson's mines.

With few experienced seamen aboard, the schooner missed the small outlet of the Klamath (above), but accidently found the Rogue River many miles north.

Five men sent ashore to investigate the area, overturned in the surf and 2 were drowned. The 3 who made their way to shore were met by waiting Indians who quickly stripped them of everything but their shirts.

Though the Indians did not otherwise harm the whites, those aboard the "Samuel Roberts," determined to save their friends, gallantly aimed the schooner's bow at the river entrance and set full sail.

The little vessel skidded across the bar and before anchors could be dropped, ground to an abrupt halt on the sandbar just beyond the river's mouth (below).

During the next 4 days short explorations were made up the Rogue River. A few miles upstream from Gold Beach on a small island called Elephant Rock (left-above), the party chiseled the year of their visit (right-above).

A careful guard was maintained during the schooner's stay in the Rogue to keep the Indians from stealing the vessel one piece at a time. Some of the enterprising tribesmen even tried to remove the ship's copper bottom sheathing with their teeth. They had made rather good progress before the activity was even noticed. One of the expedition later noted that Jefferson's Indians were at least equal to the best of the professional pick-pockets in the white man's civilization.

Convinced that the Rogue River could not provide a suitable route to the mines, the expedition sailed north. After agreeing that Coos Bay was un-satisfactory, they proceeded to Winchester Bay, which they named for one of the company.

Information from the friendly local Indians decided the party that a suitable inland route had been found. Their celebration was short-lived when they met Levi Scott and two others just completing a downstream survey of the Umpqua River. Scott had just staked out a land claim about seventeen miles upstream. It was proposed that the groups join forces and sail the "Samuel Roberts" to that point to prove the river navigable to the intended townsite.

Above Echo Island, the schooner ran aground and all parties agreed that lightening the vessel's load was the only practical means of floating free of the sand bar. The entire supply of liquor aboard was consumed to accomplish this end. With the rising tide, the schooner floated free and the location of this incident is still named "Brandy Bar".

PORTABLE IRON HOUSES,
RUST PROOF.

THE GALVANIZED IRON HOUSES

MILITARY ROADS IN SOUTHERN OREGON

The town established at the tidewater limit was named Scottsburg (left-above). The San Francisco men also chose the sites of present Elkton and Winchester to serve as trading posts along the new route. Other locations decided upon included Umpqua City on the east side of the Umpqua River, downstream from present Reedsport, and West Umpqua on the opposite river bank.

One hundred colonists with portable houses (left-center), lumber and other supplies were shipped to the new towns from San Francisco. The adventure came to an end with an Oregon legislative ruling which prohibited companies outside of the territory from holding land.

The trail between Scottsburg and Winchester became one of the major inland routes for mule pack trains. After being selected by the U.S. Army as the most suitable, it was later developed as a military route (left-below)

Only a few buildings of early Scottsburg remain (left-above). The original structures were swept away in a disastrous 1861-62 flood.

For a brief span of years, the town of Scottsburg was to be Jefferson's principal northern port of entry while at her southern boundary this same service was provided by Shasta, California (right-above).

The town of Shasta, six miles west of present Redding, became one of Jefferson's principal trading centers (left-below). Supplies from paddlewheel steamers plying the Sacramento were transferred here to the more than 2,000 pack mules and 100 freight teams for delivery to the remote mines. This abundant concentration of horse and mule population earned for Shasta the unique sobriquet, "Head of Whoa Navigation".

On their return trips the river boats carried gold dust destined for the vaults of San Francisco banks (right-below). More than $100,000 of the golden harvest made the downstream journey each week.

 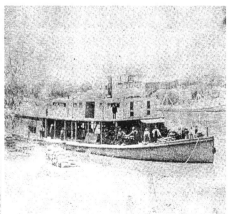

In 1853, the flimsy pine buildings of Shasta, many of which were covered or lined with cotton cloth, burned to the ground. The fire took less than half an hour to consume the entire business district. Before the ashes had cooled, new lumber was being cut to rebuild the town. To prevent a similar disaster, the new plans included many "permanent" structures.

All that remains today of old Shasta are lines of brick shells (above) and a few buildings. Among those still intact is the courthouse, now serving as a museum where the visitor can spend several pleasant hours examining the excellent display. (left-below)

Another of the structures to withstand the test of time is California's oldest Masonic Lodge, Western Star No. 2 (right-below). The hall has been in continuous operation since it was built in 1853.

As publicity was given the new mining centers (left-above) many towns sprang up. Most of these, like Bagdad (center-above) live only in the memory of the markers placed near the site of early glory.

The once booming Weaverville (right-above) is today one of the primary scenic attractions of Trinity County which it serves as county seat. The buildings with their outside circular stairways (left-below), have been carefully preserved. The court house museum displays a fine collection of relics from the early 1850's when almost half of its 3,000 population were Chinese miners.

Sawyer's Bar remains today (center-below) much as it did in 1850 (right-below). It was first called Bestville in honor of John Best, the first to discover gold at this point on the Salmon River. The community was moved three different times and was also once known as Paradise Flats.

The mule pack trains operating between the various mining camps were sometimes the means of discovery of new fields. One packer, Abraham Thompson, while leading his mule team from Oregon City to Scott Bar, camped at a point east of the present Yreka city limits in 1851. Rain had loosened the roots of the grass being contently munched by the grazing animals when Thompson noticed small particles of gold clinging to the grass ends.

The 2,000 prospectors who quickly flocked to Thompson's "Dry Diggins" (left-above) moved the principal operation to Yreka Creek because of the need for water and renamed the camp, Shasta Butte City (right-above). Confusion with the town of Shasta, however, resulted in the final adoption of the Indian term for Mount Shasta, "Wy-e-kah", which became Yreka.

In December, 1851, other mule drivers who customarily grazed their mules in the Rogue valley before starting over the Siskiyou range, discovered Rich Gulch, which first became "Table Rock" before deciding on its present identity, Jacksonville, Oregon (below).

Predating the Jacksonville strike by several months was one made by a wagon train of Illinois emigrants in Jefferson's Josephine County, Oregon.

Indians guided the party to a small stream which the whites named Josephine Creek in honor of a young daughter of one of their number, Lloyd Rollins. When the county was established in 1856, this same name was selected and remains today as Oregon's only geographic division named for a woman.

In a valley southwest of Cave Junction, rich deposits of gold were found by English sailors working their way toward Jacksonville from the coast.

By the end of 1852, a community first called Sailor Diggin's had mushroomed into a town bearing the name of Waldo (above). Once the largest business center of Josephine County, the site is today marked only by the rubble of handmade brick where a general store once stood. (left and center below).

In Waldo as in all early mining communities, the first businesses were established in tent stores with the majority of these initially serving as "refreshment" centers (right-below).

In the winter of 1852-53, the snows began to block the trails of Southern Oregon before the winter supplies could be packed in. The cost of provisions immediately rose to a new all time high, with flour at $1.00 per pound and tobacco at the same figure per ounce. The greatest demand was for salt, which was traded even for gold. Salt retained a high value until a small stream, today known as Salt Creek, on the east fork of Evans Creek, Oregon, was discovered and a cairn was erected (left-above).

A number of stage personalities of the day made the circuit of Jefferson's mining camps (right-above). One of these was a troupe which included a "child star" Lotta Crabtree. At many of her performances the western girl was showered with gold coins and nuggets by the appreciative miners.

It was claimed that at Browntown in the Democrat Gulch of Josephine County (below), she was so generously rewarded by spontaneous donations that many of her audience had to be pressed into service just to carry the gold offstage.

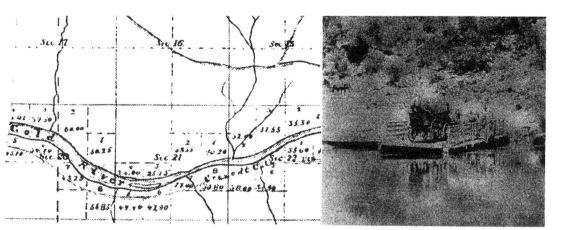

The trails through Jefferson's Rogue valley forded the Rogue River at the old Hudson's Bay crossing a few miles west of present Grants Pass. Maps of the early 1850's show the junction with the trail to the north crossing the "Gold River" (left-above). This was the name given the Rogue by the 1854 Oregon Territorial Legislature. The change was not accepted by the residents of the area and the former name was restored in 1855.

Among the first to settle in the Rogue valley was a man named Long who built a barge of logs controlled by ropes and a rudder by which the swift current caused the ferry to be propelled to the opposite bank (right-above). Fee charges were paid in "pinches" of gold.

In 1851, the ferry was sold to James Tufts and James Vannoy and they posted the following rates for crossing charges:

Unloaded wagon	$1.00
Loaded	1.50
Yoke of oxen	.25
1 sheep or hog	.25
Any other loaded animal	.25
Unloaded	.12½

Foot passengers same as unloaded animals.

A competitive ferry was operated by Davis Evans. It was located near the mouth of the creek which bears his name in the town of Rogue River, Oregon. Another ferryman was Joel Perkins who built the valley's first cabin and sawmill a mile east of present Grants Pass.

Rough and unfair treatment of the Indians by some of the miners often resulted in the death of innocent victims who had the misfortune to be in the area when the tribes determined to obtain revenge, and all packers travelling the Rogue valley trail kept their weapons in readiness (below).

General Joseph Lane, a hero of the Mexican War, had been appointed first Territorial Governor of Oregon in 1849. In May, 1850, he left Oregon City with a party of 15 whites and 15 Klickitat Indians to try their hand in Jefferson's mines. Lane's successor, John Gaines, had not yet taken office, and it was Lane's plan to make a treaty with the Takelma tribe of the Rogue valley on his way to Shasta valley.

The Takelmas had attacked a party of miners at Rocky Point, near present Gold Hill. After taking what they considered of value, they had dumped the rest of the booty, including bags of "yellow dust" into the river.

The first treaty meeting took place near the mouth of present Bear Creek in the south side of the Rogue River (left-below). Lane displayed amazing bravery in single-handedly striking bows and arrows from the hands of some 75 warriors who violated the meeting agreement by coming armed. This act so impressed the chief Apsakahah (Horserider) that he asked Lane for permission to use the name of Jo and agreed to the terms of the treaty as proposed.

Despite the treaty, attacks and reprisals continued throughout the Rogue valley until the whites sent messengers north to the closest military post, Fort Vancouver (right-below). On the way they met two companies of mounted riflemen enroute to Fort Benicia, California. Armed forces in the Pacific Northwest were being reduced in number because Oregon's Territorial delegate to Congress, Samuel Thurston, had publicly stated that the Indians of Oregon were friendly and troops were no longer needed.

Phil Kearney, the leading officer of the "Mounted Rifles", split his detachment into two groups to attack an Indian encampment near Bear Creek. In the action, Captain James Stuart was killed by a poisoned arrow and buried on a knoll in today's Central Point, which the soldiers named for the captain. Within two years' the name had been changed from Camp Stuart to Bear Creek by the settlers of the valley.

Joined by some thirty miners, Kearney made three attacks on the main Indian encampment at the north side of Table Rock but was driven back each time. Chief Jo of the Takelmas answered a demand for surrender with the boast that he could keep a thousand arrows in the air at all times.

After four days of fighting, the Indians withdrew and were trailed up Sardine Creek where they entirely eluded the troops and volunteers, who took as hostages about thirty Takelma women and children.

Anxious to continue on to Benicia, Kearney turned the hostages over to Joseph Lane, who had joined the volunteers. Lane in turn gave them to Governor Gaines at Vannoy Crossing. Gaines had hurried south without escort when word of the uprising had reached Oregon City. Gaines used the captured Indians to deal with the tribes in concluding a new treaty.

As a result of the 1851 problems and the constant attacks of the Modocs on emigrant trains near Tule Lake, Major Fitzgerald was sent with a company of dragoons to establish a military post in Jefferson. The sites chosen was the Scott valley of California and the post was named Fort Jones (above).

During its active use (1852-1858), the fort served as a training outpost for many officers of both Union and Confederate forces, whose names had become immortal even before the old fort fell to ruin (left-below).

Fort Reading in Trinity County was the next army post established in 1852 and named in honor of P. B. Reading, discoverer of gold in Jefferson. The fort saw service until a malaria outbreak caused it to be abandoned in favor of Fort Crook in Fall River, California (right-below). The latter, in turn, gave way to Bidwell in Modoc County in 1869.

The steam propellor driven "Sea Gull" under Captain William Tichenor, stopped at Port Orford on its regularly scheduled run between San Francisco and Portland in 1851. Following a U. S. Navy order to explore the area for a possible inland mail route, J. M. Kirkpatrick and 8 others were set ashore. The expedition was equipped with a 5 lb. saluting cannon, small arms, tools, and provisions. They were greeted by Indians who seemed quite friendly until the "Sea Gull", which was to return in two weeks with additional supplies had departed from the bay.

After the ship's departure, the Indians began to gather and their general attitude caused the whites to move their equipment to a rock island about 100 yards from shore, which was accessible only at low tide.

The following morning the Indians made a surprise attack. Kirkpatrick seized a burning log from the fire and ignited the charge of the small cannon which had been loaded for the emergency. Confused by the loud explosion, the Indians retreated and left 20 of their dead behind (left-below).

After another attack had been driven off, the Indian chief came out on the beach, threw down his arms and asked to be allowed to remove his dead. Kirkpatrick agreed to this and advised the chief that he and his men would depart in 14 days when the "Sea Gull" returned. The "Sea Gull" did not appear on schedule, however, and the Indians, who had observed the truce for 15 days, attacked until the whites had nearly exhausted their ammunition.

The exploring party abandoned the rocks under cover of darkness and made their way north to Umpqua City. The details of the attack are outlined on the Battle Rock monument, which is located on the south side of present Port Orford (right-below).

Captain Tichenor, whose delay had been caused by a legal seizure of the "Sea Gull" in San Francisco, returned aboard the "Columbia" the day after the Kirkpatrick party had left. After viewing the scene he was certain that the entire party had been killed. With the "Columbia's" return, the Alta California carried the story of the party's massacre (left-above).

A new group under James Gable sailed from San Francisco on the "Sea Gull's" next trip and built a stockade of heavy logs at present Point Orford, which they named Fort Point.

Tichenor advertised in San Francisco papers that he could land men within 30 miles of a new gold discovery at Big Bar near present Gold Hill. About 40 men answered the offer, and William Green T'Vault who had just returned from guiding Kearney to Benicia was hired to lead the party inland. Horses and supplies were landed. T'Vault took 20 men and started out to find the new route to the Rogue valley.

They moved south to the north bank of the Rogue which they followed upstream for about 50 miles. Here the rugged terrain discouraged half of the party, who retraced their steps back to the coast.

The remaining explorers turned north and became completely lost. Abandoning their horses, they started to follow a small stream which became the Coquille River.

About 2 miles from the ocean, they found Indian villages on each side of the river a short distance from present Bandon, Oregon.

As the party stepped ashore, the Indians attacked and killed all but 5 of the whites. Three of these escaped north to the Umpqua settlement while T'Vault and a companion managed to return to Fort Point.

As a result of these attacks, the army established Fort Orford as a military post in 1852.

The fuse which ingnited the Indian temper was the 1853 Jacksonville hanging of an innocent Indian youngster who had been the guiltless spectator to the hanging of two Shastas accused of killing a Thomas Wells.

The Indians repaid this injustice by burning 10 homes. Word of the outbreak was sent to Forts Orford, Vancouver, and Jones, and the plea for help was first answered by Capt. Bradley Alden who brought a force of ten men with him from Fort Jones. These regulars were soon joined at Jacksonville by 150 volunteers from Yreka and Joseph Lane accompanied by neighbors from the area of present Roseburg.

While the whites were organizing, a pitched battle took place near Williams, Oregon, and the stockade of Alberding and Dunn near Ashland was attacked.

Lane was given command of the forces and patrols were assigned the task of finding the main body of Indians who had left their Table Rock encampment.

Following an attack on one of the patrols near Evans Creek, the Indians were trailed to the east slope of Battle Mountain where they had built a crude log fort.

Captain Alden led the first assault but was seriously wounded when he bent over to pick up a ramrod. Pleasant Armstrong, one of the builders of the "Star of Oregon" whose name appears on the 1843 Champoeg roster, was among the first three killed.

Lane, who had also been wounded, called for a cease fire until the terms of the treaty could be discussed.

On Sept. 10, 1953, a treaty meeting was held in a clearing near the winter quarters of the Takelmas at the north side of Table Rock (below).

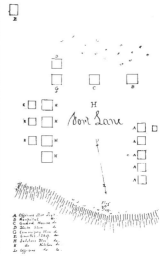

Residents of the Willamette valley, who greatly respected Pleasant Armstrong, sent a zinc casket to Jacksonville to return his remains for more proper interment than had been provided at the site of the conflict at Battle Mountain. The heavy casket, carried up the rugged terrain, was left tied to a pine tree (left-above). The 3 bodies of the common grave were found to be "too ripe" to determine which one had been Armstrong. Pieces of the casket may be seen in the Jacksonville Museum, and the beautiful Pleasant Valley and Creek perpetuate this famous pioneer's memory.

The 1853 Indian War terminated with the establishment of the Table Rock Reservation. Samuel Colver, whose home still stands in Phoenix, Oregon (center-above) was named as Indian Agent.

The reservation post, Fort Lane (right-above) was built between the Reservation and the emigrant road through the Rogue valley.

The location chosen for Fort Lane was on a knoll to the south of Table Rock, which can be located today by a marker placed about 200 yds. from the actual site of the fort (right-center).

The post was built by Capt. Andrew Jackson Smith who had been sent from Fort Orford in response to the request for help. Smith's force of 60 dragoons, like that of August Kantz, arrived with a 12 lb. howitzer, too late to be of service in the Battle Mountain fight.

Surrounded by a reservation of 640 acres, the fort included separate log buildings for the officers (right-below) and soldiers' quarters, a bakery, kitchens, storerooms, hospital, blacksmith shop, and a guardhouse.

A few miners had discovered gold in the ocean beach sand north of the Coquille River in 1852 but kept their find secret. Capt. A. J. Smith, in an official military report, mentioned he had found traces of the metal near Fort Orford before before being called to the Rogue valley. By mid 1854, the town of Randolph (left-above) was established north of present Bandon and a thousand miners had set up sluice boxes lined with quicksilver to capture the fine gold carried to the ocean by coastal streams and washed back upon the shores by the tides (right-above).

The beach mining operations extended to the shores south of the mouth of the Rogue River where present Gold Beach is now located.

The name of Gold Beach was derived from the early mining activity, the town having been originally named Ellensburg in honor of the wife of Capt. Tichenor who had taken up residence at Fort Orford.

During 1854, a figure who would later appear in a great role upon the American scene, Captain Hiram Ulysses Simpson Grant, was transferred to Fort Humbolt near present Eureka, California (below) from Fort Vancouver, Washington. The man who was later to become president found the army post life so dull that his chief occupation became the reduction of Ryan's Saloon whiskey inventory, at which job he was so successful that his resignation from the army was requested.

Fort Humboldt near Eureka.

The first serious effort of Jefferson's rapidly growing number of citizens to establish statehood began with a bill introduced in the 1852 California state legislature at Vallejo, California (left-above) to form a "State of Shasta". The reasons for this move were numerous and varied.

Early settlers had been deeply impressed by Jefferson's ability to sustain itself solely on its own resources, but were distressed by the high taxes, poor mail service and the lack of military protection.

The joining of forces to combat the Indian tribes had established a common bond between the residents on both sides of the Siskiyous, and out of these wars had emerged a feeling of "oneness" which could never be separated by a man-conceived boundary.

The State of Shasta died in legislative committee only because of the pressure of other business at that session.

That following year at the New State House at Benicia (right-above)

another attempt to form a new state was made, now bearing the name, "State of Klamath".

The Daily Alta California of San Francisco, December 19, 1853, pleaded the cause of the new state with: "Southern Oregon and Northern California . . . embracing the range of country east of the coast and stretching from Cape Mendecino to the Umpqua heads (about the same length as the present state of Washington), presents a country of uniform character and is distinct from the rest of either California or Oregon.

"It is necessary to form it into a state by itself and have its interests fairly represented in the United States Congress. Its interests are separate and distinct and clogs the administration of both.

"Let our local resources be developed by a government identified with our locality; let us have a voice in the national councils where we can urge upon Congress our wants".

Another December issue of the Alta California reported: "Crescent City is prosperous and hopes to become the capital of the new State of Klamath".

The plan was supported by the 1853 Yreka Herald which pointed out that California planned no development of Jefferson because the area was "of too secondary a nature to receive any effective support from the people of Oregon and California or from their delegation in Congress".

The article went on to substantiate the Alta California claims with: "Southern Oregon and Northern California . . . present . . . country of uniform character and (are) distinct from the rest of either California or Oregon. Therefore let the people speak out and unite upon some plan of action for the purpose of forming a new territory of Northern California and Southern Oregon".

The interior of the reconstructed Ben-

icia Statehouse (above) looks much as it did in 1853. The ceiling supports were from masts of San Francisco's stranded sailing fleet.

Of the many attempts to establish separate statehood, the most serious of the earnest efforts was made in 1854. The Yreka Herald of December 30, 1853, issued a call for a mass meeting of Jefferson's citizens at Jacksonville, Oregon "for the purpose of taking into consideration the propriety of organizing a new territory (to be called Jackson), and to devise means to effect the same".

This meeting was called to order in the Robinson House, on Saturday, January 7, 1854. L. F. Mosher, son-in-law of the famed General Joseph Lane, presided over the historic conclave which concluded with plans for a general convention to be held with delegates representing all southern Oregon and northern California counties.

The second meeting was also held at Dr. Jesse Robinson's hotel (left-above), which stood on the same site at Jacksonville's recently restored United States Hotel (right-above). At this time, H. G. Ferris, of Siskiyou County, California, was elected President pro tem, and Elisha Steele of Yreka shared vice-presidential honors with Samuel Colver of Phoenix, Oregon. T. McFadden Patton and Charles S. Drew from Jacksonville served jointly in the office of secretary.

Prominent political leaders from Oregon's Coos and Douglas (then Umpqua) counties, had responded to the meeting call and were counted with delegates representing most of the northern California region.

The convention prepared individual resolutions for their respective legislatures in Oregon and California and drafted the following memorial to the United States Congress: "Whereas, the Legislative Assembly of the Territory of Oregon have introduced and passed an act for the consent of the people of said territory to be taken in reference to the formation of a state government, therefore Resolved, that we will use every exertion to prevent the formation of a state government in Oregon with its present boundaries . . . "

The memorial was presented at the 33rd Congress by Lane, then Oregon's Territorial Representative. He forwarded a personal note to the Jacksonville "malecontents" that he did not personally favor the secession effort. Lane feared that the time needed to complete the work of forming an additional territory at this time would endanger and delay his plans for the admission of Oregon to which task he had been previously committed.

The very same newspapers which recorded the new territorial plan carried the first mention of a new series of Indian troubles which were to place the stamp of failure upon the entire effort.

The Oregon Statesman.
OFFICIAL PAPER OF THE TERRITORY.

TUESDAY, FEBRUARY 7, 1854.

[The upper portion of the page reproduces columns of the newspaper "The Oregon Statesman" of February 7, 1854, including legislative proceedings ("IN THE COUNCIL, Jan. 31"), an editorial "For the States—New Office, &c.", a resolution of the House of Representatives of the Territory of Oregon, correspondence dated "JACKSONVILLE, Jan. 18, 1854," "YREKA, Saturday, Jan. 14," "COTTONWOOD, January 14," a notice "AN ESTRAY LAW," and an item headed "New Territory" reporting a meeting at the Robinson House in Jacksonville, Jan. 7, signed SAMUEL COLVER, Pres't, T. McF. Patton, Sec'y. The small type is largely illegible.]

In the Oregon Statesman (above) news column immediately following the convention report, appeared the story of a battle near present Hornbrook, California, between some fifty Shastas under Chief Bill and a combined force of volunteers and regular troops from forts Lane and Jones.

Though the threat of renewed hostilities caused the Oregon delegation to withdraw from further active participation in the "Jackson Territory" move, California groups continued their efforts when their legislature refused to improve the northern roads.

The Shasta Courier of April 28, 1855 complained: "The manner in which the claims of the North . . . is ignored by the California legislature, would be laughable, were it not for the fact that the wrong thereby inflicted upon us is too great for our outraged feelings to find expression in other than bitter and indignant terms . . . ".

This outburst was followed by the May 12, 1855 issue stating that taxable property in the proposed territory was currently valued at 7 million dollars from which taxes of $41,156 could be anticipated. Additional revenue, the article contended, would be provided by foreign miners' (Chinese, in particular) licenses and poll taxes totaling $48,756. The sum of all sources of potential revenue would provide an annual figure of $100,000, an amount more than sufficiently adequate to cover the costs of maintaining local government.

Had Jefferson's citizens been allowed to continue at this crucial point in negotiations, history might have recorded the emergence of the embryonic "Jackson Territory" in the mid 1850's, but the stage for the final major Indian resistance had already been set.

Part VIII
The Indian Resistance

The creation of Washington Territory in 1853 had alerted the tribes of that area as well as those in Jefferson to the danger of the final overwhelming invasion of land hungry white settlers. Yakima Chief, Kamiakin, called a major war council at the Grand Ronde Valley in eastern Oregon in 1854. This was the greatest assembly of Indian nations ever known in the Pacific Northwest, and lasted 5 days with tribal representatives from northern California to Canada in attendance. It was here decided that the first action against the Yakimas would be the signal for a simultaneous uprising to drive the whites from the Northwest.

When Major Granville Haller entered the Simcoe Mountain territory of the Yakimas, Kamiakin attacked, and signal fires blazed atop mountain peaks from upper Washington to central California. On October 8, 1855, Major J. A. Lupton and a company of 30 men struck a village of Takelma women,

children and old men at the mouth of Little Butte Creek in Southern Oregon.

The following day Indian raiding parties began a systematic attack by killing a teamster and the members of a pack train a few miles from Jacksonville. Working north along the emigrant road, they killed all the whites they encountered and burned all houses but two between Jacksonville and Grave Creek.

At Harris Flat, north of Grants Pass, George Harris was fatally wounded as he entered his cabin, and Mrs. Harris, in one of the most dramatic actions of Oregon history, held off the Indians with the help of her wounded daughter. Firing the family guns from different points in the cabin, she was able to make the raiders believe that the cabin had a considerable number of defenders. Today she lies buried beside her first husband in the quiet Jacksonville cemetery (left-below). Her picture and one of the weapons used in her heroic stand are displayed at the Jacksonville museum (right-below).

Merlin Galice Stage
1908

The Harris boy, 10 year old David, had gone to visit the Haines home at present Merlin, where the Rogue valley's oldest apple tree still marks the cabin site (left-above). His fate and that of Mrs. Haines and her eldest daughter was never established.

The first major clash with the tribes was at the site of Galice(right-above). Having warning of the coming attack by an Indian known to the whites as Umpqua Joe the small settlement was able to hold off the Indians, though about a third of the miners were killed. Many lost their lives trying to extinquish fires set by flaming arrows, which burned all buildings of the community except that in which the besieged company had forted up.

Shortly after this action, a patrol from Fort Orford discovered a major concentration of Indians near the mouth of Galice Creek and a battalion of about 250 regulars and volunteers set out over the Indian trail toward the Indian encampment. The tangled underbrush had been made nearly impassable by trees felled across the trail. When one such tree was accidently set afire, the hope of surprising the Indians was lost.

The Indians were awaiting the troops on a hill (left-below), over which the trail passed after crossing a brushy ravine. From behind the outcropping of huge boulders a man could stand erect and view anyone approaching on the trail for many miles (right-below).

Behind their rock cover, the Indians were almost completely protected from the bullets of the whites.

When the military made its disastrous charge, the Indian guns, superior to the smooth bore army issue musketoon, picked off the troops in such numbers that the latter had to withdraw.

The injuries of the wounded so contaminated the water of the creek by which the soldiers set up camp, that the place was named Bloody Spring. With nothing to eat during the siege, the troops called the fortified area Hungry Hill and retreated with their wounded (left-above) to the field hospital set up at Fort Birdseye, east of the present town of Rogue River (right-above).

After the battle of Hungry Hill, stockades were erected at Vannoy's ferry (left-below) and at the Harkness and Twogood tavern at Grave Creek (right-below) in anticipation of Indian attacks.

Because of its central location, Fort Vannoy became the principal base of operations for the volunteer forces. The regular troops made their headquarters at Fort Lane.

While the whites were gathering strength for a major campaign, the warring tribes were busy making raids on scattered settlements in which they burned houses in the Jump-off Joe Creek region and attacked the Table Rock Reservation of Chief Sam, who refused to break his 1853 treaty.

At the site of Steamboat in Jackson County, Chief John and his band were discovered living in log cabins abandoned by the miners. After sending for reinforcements and a howitzer from Fort Lane the volunteers attacked. The mule hauling the cannon lost its footing in the six inches of early January snow and was drowned in a creek.

The battle continued for 4 days until the howitzer and dry powder could be brought up. When finally mounted, it was fired all afternoon with only one shell ever hitting the cabins. The exploding ball killed two warriors and two children. The fighting continued until nightfall. Even though completely surrounded by posted guards, the Indians withdrew through the white lines during the night. Their wounded left a trail of blood clearly visible on the snow in the daylight of the following day.

Many headstones in the Rogue valley mark the graves of those killed during the 1855-56 conflict.

Martin Angel (left-below) was shot while enroute to the Steamboat battle, and William Guest (center-below) was killed with his own gun while plowing his field with an ox team.

McDonaugh Harkness (right-below), who had been present at an 1853 killing of six Indians at the Bates house on Grave Creek, was ambushed while carrying dispatches from Leland to Little Meadows. His body was mutilated by tribesmen and his heart hung from a bush. All of the parts which could be found were buried in the Croxton Cemetery of Grants Pass.

that If can gather that Enos the notorious robber has ... 30 or 50 Indians with him it at his command that wont leave this section of the country. I would suggest that there be a reward offered for Enos dead or alive as he is beyond a doubt an outlaw and all his party as their chiefs have located and left the country I think if a liberal reward was offered for those outlaws that there would be men enough that would soon close the present difficultys. I would suggest that one thousand dollars be offered for Enos dead or alive and two hundred apiece for the others dead or alive I suppose that they all would have to be taken dead unless it

A Washington Day ball at Gold Beach was interrupted by the attack of Indians led by a Canadian half-breed, one-time guide of the John Fremont party, named Enos. A reward of $1,000 had been offered for the capture of Enos in the Illinois Valley (above).

At the time of the attack in which 60 homes from Big Bend of the Rogue River to Gold Beach were burned and 31 settlers killed, the Indian agent, Ben Wright had made a trip to one of the Indian villages to arrest Enos, and was killed with an axe. In admiration of Wright's bravery against the Modocs at the time of the Bloody Point (Klamath County) wagon train incidents, his heart was removed and eaten. Wright's Indian wife, Chetco Jenny, participated in the ceremony.

A fortification at Gold Beach was hastily completed and named Miner's Fort. The 130 men, women and children of the area moved in for what was to become a full month's siege.

Thirty-five miners from the Chetco River area set out to aid the Gold Beach defenders but were attacked at Pistol River (left-below). They were rescued by troops from Fort Humbolt after three days of fighting. The troops and miners then marched north to relieve Miner's Fort.

A few days later, Fort Hays (right-below) was attacked. A battle which included many hand to hand combats was carried on far into the night. It resumed the following day near the base of Eight Dollar Mountain and ended with the whites being driven back to the safety of Fort Hays.

OREGON HISTORY
THE BATTLE OF PISTOL RIVER
SEVERE FIGHTING TOOK PLACE IN CURRY COUNTY DURING THE LAST ROGUE RIVER INDIAN WAR. IN MARCH 1856 A COMPANY OF MINUTE MEN 34 STRONG UNDER COMMAND OF GEORGE H. ABBOTT WERE BESIEGED IN AN IMPROVISED FORTIFICATION OF LOGS BY A LARGE FORCE OF PISTOL RIVER AND ROGUE RIVER INDIANS. THE INDIANS CONTRARY TO THEIR USUAL CUSTOM REPEATEDLY CHARGED WITH DESPERATE COURAGE. THE SIEGE INVOLVING HAND TO HAND FIGHTING WAS CARRIED ON FOR SEVERAL DAYS UNTIL THE INDIANS WERE FINALLY DISPERSED BY REGULAR TROOPS UNDER CAPTAINS ORD AND JONES.

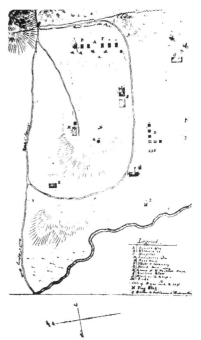

The war plan of the military was to drive the Indians away from the Rogue valley settlements toward Gold Beach and into the guns of Fort Humbolt troops moving up the Rogue River.

Captain Smith was sent from Fort Lane to join the regulars near Agness, Oregon, while the volunteers forced the Indians down river.

Among the monuments marking the Indian uprising on the Oregon coast is one in memory of the Geisal family (left-above) who had ignored the warning of an Indian woman on the afternoon of the attack. Mrs. Geisal and her 13 year old daughter were taken captive but returned unharmed, though against the wishes of a chief who claimed the young girl as his property.

About 1,300 Indians were rounded up and held at Fort Orford, from where they were shipped to the Siletz Reservation on the southern end of the 70 mile long tract along the Oregon coast bounded on the north by the Grande Ronde Reservation (right-above).

The Grand Ronde Reserve had already received Chief Sam and his people, who had never broken the treaty of 1853. Being in constant danger from both the warring tribes and vengeful whites, Sam had requested that his people be taken to another reserve until the end of the war. With a guard of 100 soldiers to prevent attack from the Willamette valley settlers, the entire tribe was moved to the Yamhill River valley even though heavy snows fell throughout the entire trip north.

Near Illahee, Oregon, Captain Smith and his 80 dragoons were engaged in battle with Chief John and over a third of the troopers were killed. During the 2 night siege, tribesmen scaled the steep cliff to the knoll (left-above) where Smith's men had dug trenches (right-above) with their mess gear, to steal blankets from the sleeping soldiers.

On the meadow below the hill where Smith had made his stand, a final battle between the massed troops and regulars and the tribes under Chief John ended in a rout of Indians. Terms of a treaty had been dictated to Chief John by Superintendent of Indian Affairs Joel Palmer several days before at Oak Flat (left-below).

John himself was the last to surrender and picked up his gun twice before at last reluctantly joining his warriors to end the final organized resistance of the Rogue River tribes on June 29, 1856.

Enos was hanged at Fort Orford for the murder of Ben Wright amid full ceremony as was justified by the occasion.

The new reserve was established on the Siletz River in Lincoln County (right-below). To prevent the tribes from returning to their southern Oregon home, three forts were constructed, bounding the Siletz and Grande Ronde reservations. The southernmost of these was Fort Umpqua, and located near the northwestern boundary of Jefferson's domain at Winchester Bay.

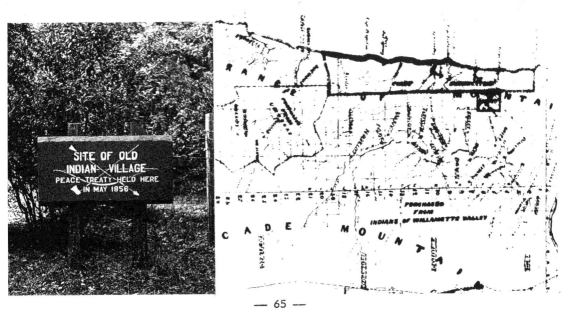

A new Fort Umpqua (left-above) was erected on the east bank of the Umpqua River near the site of the early town started by the Klamath Expedition of 1850. On the routes into the Willamette valley, Fort Hoskins in Benton County and Fort Yamhill (right-above) near the present Valley Junction were built by Phillip Sheridan. This latter blockhouse may be viewed today at Dallas, Oregon (left-below).

Life on the reservation during the first year was not a happy one, and the hasty shelters they set up provided little protection from the heavy rainfall and damp climate of the coastal range. Sections of the reserve were sold by unscrupulous agents, one of whom complained bitterly of his meager pay while amassing a personal account of $40,000 during his four years of service.

Due to the skillful maneuvering of the whites, the Indians were fortunate to receive even $80,000 of the $250,000 appropriated by Congress.

The failures to keep treaty agreements made Chief John justifiably bitter and he tried to arouse his warriors into making a break from the reservation.

John and his son were ordered to be taken to Fort Alcatraz military prison in San Francisco Bay. Aboard the "Columbia" (right-below) they tried to make their escape when the vessel was near Humbolt Bay. While attempting to steal the gun of their soldier guard John became over-enthusiastic and gave a war whoop, which aroused the crew and passengers. In the fight that followed, several passengers were wounded, and John's son, George, lost a leg from a blow with a butcher's meat cleaver.

After a confinement of several years, the two were released and returned to the reservation where John "could see again his wife and daughters who tend upon him and comb his hair".

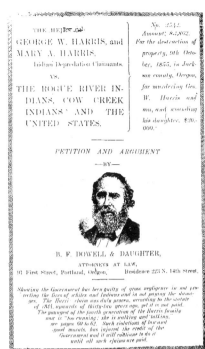

A few Indians, because of their efforts to help the whites during the uprising, were allowed to remain in Jefferson's settlements and some attempt was made to reward their services.

Klamath Peggy, who had walked 20 miles of rugged mountain trails over Humbug Mountain to warn the Yreka citizens of a planned attack by the Klamaths, was given a small pension by the Californians for the remainder of her days.

Umpqua Joe, whose warning had given the miners time to prepare for the attack at Galice, took up land near the present Bridge below Hell's Gate on the Rogue and operated a ferry (left-above). This property was officially given to his daughter Mary in 1885 by the United States in an act which created the smallest Indian reservation in America.

By the time peace had been restored to the Rogue valley, statehood for Oregon had been virtually assured.

The war had cost over 6 million dollars. This had been borne principally by the settlers with less than half that amount actually returned by the government. Some claims, such as that for the death of George Harris (right-above) were approved by Congress but never paid.

The remote possibility that the new state of Oregon would be able to apply congressional pressure to fully reimburse the settlers' losses made the supporters of "Jackson Territory" hesitant to resume further action and the effort was once more set aside.

With the close of the 1855-56 Indian War, the citizens of Jefferson living north of the Siskiyous resumed the task of building new industries to augment the economic growth previously based solely on the area's mineral wealth.

To further discourage Indian uprisings, Lt. Crook, later to achieve national fame by his capture of Geronimo, was ordered to establish a fort near the Klamath River's mouth.

In October, 1857, Crook and a company of 52 men built Fort Ter-Waw about six miles upriver from the mouth of the Klamath. A small sawmill set up to cut the lumber for some 25 buildings which included storehouses, barracks and officer's quarters.

The Indian word Ter-Waw for which the post was named meant a "pretty" or "nice" place and was one well chosen to describe this northern region of the State of Jefferson's giant redwood groves.

The serious statehood attempt in the mid 1850's had been based partially upon the condition of Jefferson's roads and with the Indian problems temporarily eased, improvement of these vital links between Oregon and California was given a high priority.

In the good old Yankee tradition of private enterprise and sheer determination, the first highways were nearly all privately financed toll roads (left-below).

Wm. Lowden built his first road in 1858 between Weaverville and Shasta without the aid of modern earthmovers while skeptics acidly predicted that every foot of the project would cost more than two or three hundred dollars. The 24½ mile road from the Tower House (right-below) to Weaverville was completed for about $20,000.

Part IX
The "Six Horse Limited" Stagecoach

By 1858 the Pioneer Wagon Road from Crescent City to Jacksonville had succeeded the 1853 Cold Spring Mountain Trail established by the early packers.

In this same decade, the forerunner of present U. S. Highway 5 across the Siskiyou Mountains was opened with the linking of Coles Station and Ashland by the Siskiyou Toll Road (above).

Many of the early routes through Jefferson (right) had been established by the Army. The road between the Rogue valley and Scottsburg was one of these which was constructed by "Fighting Joe" Hooker of later Civil War fame.

The problem of maintaining the roads was solved in part by a road tax which could be paid by a given amount of physical labor or the hiring of some other person to do the required repair work. Since inexpensive Chinese labor was readily available in many of the areas, actual cash rarely found its way to the public coffers.

Completion of these "improved" highways heralded the beginning of the northwest stagecoach era which was to endure throughout the span of years between 1859 and 1887.

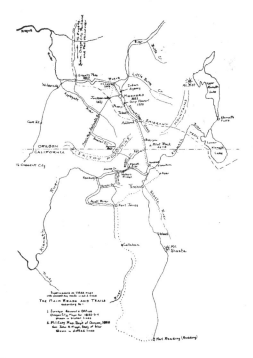

The Oregon and Shasta Express (left-above) had been placed in operation by W. G. T'Vault in 1852. This service with its rather indefinite running schedule between Yreka, California, and Winchester, Oregon, struggled along until the beginning of a weekly run between Salem and Jacksonville.

By 1850, the California Oregon Stage Company (center-above) had expanded its service to Oakland, Oregon, where the Chase Line operated to Corvallis. Here the passengers and cargo transferred to the Oregon Stage Co. to reach Portland.

The six horse Concord coach which has been immortalized in literature and legends of the west, was first placed in operation on the Pacific coast by the California Stage Company.

The Concord stage was a work of superb hand craftsmanship by the New England firm of Abbott, Downing, and Co. (right-below). With an immense pair of leather sling rockers connecting the coach body to its running gear, the unit rode much like a swinging cradle. In these days before sea sickness pills many passengers found the long journeys a definite challenge.

On the right outside seat was the driver and in good weather a chosen passenger was privileged to sit between him and the "Shotgun Messenger" protecting the treasure box and mail. These items were carried beneath the driver's seat in the front "boot" or leather laced waterproof oil-cloth cover. Another large boot of waterproof canvas, reinforced with leather straps, was mounted at the rear of the coach to protect the passengers' baggage against rain and splashing of creek crossings.

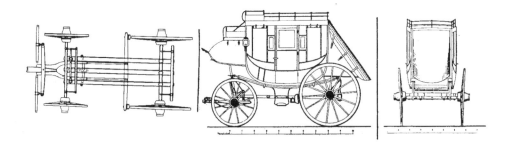

The California Stage presented an interesting color scheme study. Wheels, tongue and other running gear were painted a bright chrome yellow and outlined with black stripes through which were spaced single red roses. The body was olive green with large hand painted landscape scenes on the panels.

White horses were most commonly used (above), and their black harnesses were adorned with silver buckles. Around the neck of each horse was a chain made of ivory rings, every other link being stained a brilliant red, from which hung a pendant with the trademark of the O & C Stage Co., a silver wreath formed by a stage driver's whip mounted on an ivory background.

The coach was equipped with three seats, each of which could carry three passengers.

The drivers of the stage, not to be outdone by its eye-catching appearance, often wore fine buckskin gloves or gauntlets decorated with fancy stitching to match the silk cracker of his whip-lash. Expensive, well-made boots were given a high polish to catch the public eye as the foot brakes were applied. The driver's hat was usually a round, low crown gray felt with a medium brim. His three cornered neckerchief prevented a collar chafed neck in winter or served as a mask against the summer dust.

No story of the stagecoach days could be considered complete without mention of those adventurers who believed that the living due them should come from the treasure chests of stageline operators like Wells and Fargo. Most holdups were conducted on the steep mountain passes up which the coaches moved at no more than a slow walk.

For eight long years, Jefferson's lawmen scoured the country for a bold highway man who had assumed the name of Black Bart the Po8 (poet). The mild appearing Charles E. Boles (left-below) usually left mocking verses at the scene of each of his 28 successful holdups (center-below) and was responsible for the greatest number of reward posters (right-below) printed by Wells-Fargo.

Boles was captured after being traced through a laundry mark on his handkerchief left near Copperopolis. The arresting law officers found a suitcase with the disassembled shotgun used by Bart throughout his career. No shells could be found and the ever polite highwayman explained that he never owned ammunition because he did not want anyone to "get hurt". The gun, he said, was only carried "for effect".

Among the more noted of Jefferson's stage drivers operating out of Sacramento was "One Eyed Charlie" Parkhurst (left-above), who died in 1879 after more than 30 years of the jolting service. "Charlie's" checkered career included the thwarting of an attempted holdup of the Wells Fargo cash cargo and the loss of at least one day's work each month from the effects of a payday hang-over. An increase in the wad of chewing tobacco in "Charlie's" cheek was considered by travelers to be an accurate indication of a rougher road ahead.

With the death of Parkhurst, it was discovered that the stager was a woman and her personal effects revealed the given name of Charlotte. Since she had cast a ballot in 1868, she held the distinction of being the first U. S. woman to vote. Being a member in good standing, she was buried in the Odd Fellows Cemetery at Watsonville, California (right-above).

Though a great multitude of stage stations once served Jefferson's north-south traffic, only a few have survived the ravages of time. Excellent examples of these early hostelries are Callahan's Ranch near Etna, California (left-below), and Southern Oregon's Wolf Creek Tavern (right-below).

Part X
The Civil War Years

Through the pre-Civil War years the most vociferous supporters of the Southern cause were spread through Jefferson's southern Oregon counties.

When the clouds of war finally released their terrible fury, secret Confederate organizations bearing the names, "Knights of the Golden Circle" and "Friends of the Union" met more openly in Jacksonville than in any other western seaboard community.

Jefferson's secessionists heartily supported the "Pacific Republic" plan and they were joined, at least in spirit and sympathy, by some disgruntled proponents of the mid 1850 "State of Jackson" effort.

Hopes for separate statehood had not been completely erased during the last of the pre-war years. Though an effort by Jefferson's coastal towns to arouse interest in a "Coos Territory" did not progress beyond the discussion stage, the possibility of Jefferson's secession remained a strong possibility throughout the war.

To forestall any actual outbreak by Jefferson's "Rebs", Camp Lincoln near Crescent City, California (left-below), and Baker at Phoenix, Oregon (right-below), were established as recruiting and training points for Federal forces. Flanked on the east and west by these posts, Southern Oregon's Confederate sympathizers were easily held in check.

Most of the Union Army Volunteer forces recruited in California and Oregon spent their Civil War years patrolling the roads between Jefferson and the new mining discovery towns of Idaho, Washington and Nevada.

During these years Indian uprisings plagued Jefferson from Humboldt Bay to the Nevada border. In one of the many battles and skirmishes that took place, George Crook engaged, and finally defeated, a strongly entrenched tribe in their rock fortifications at the Infernal Caverns Battleground south of Alturas.

A Confederate plot to capture the Benecia arsenal, Alcatraz and Fort Point (left-above) was uncovered with the capture of a hidden crew aboard the schooner "J. W. Chapman" (right-below). The ship, with cannon and munitions in her hold was seized trying to leave San Francisco Bay. Had the venture succeeded, the "Chapman" would have been used to raid the Pacific coast sea lanes for the Confederacy.

Among the ringleaders who had devised the plot were some of Jefferson's "Pacific Republic" supporters.

A baby civil war erupted within Jefferson's borders in 1863. Historians have recorded this action as the "Sagebrush War".

The Honey Lake valley of California had, since 1856, been claimed by both the Nevada Territory and California. Susanville, which had its beginning as a mining claim of Isaac Roop from Shasta and a group of prospectors under Peter Lassen, was the scene of an election in 1862 in which two sets of officials, one representing California and the other Nevada, were simultaneously elected to preside over the same area.

The elected California sheriff set out to arrest the Nevada representation of law and order. The latter had with him some 35 followers and had assembled at Roop's cabin which they renamed "Fort Defiance" (below). The "Never Sweats" as the Nevada miners were called, opened fire when the Californians approached.

Reinforcements for both sides continued to arrive throughout the 24 hour battle and by the next evening this minature civil war was beginning to assume the proportions of its eastern counterpart.

An armistice was called until the state boundaries could be determined and the resultant survey placed the area in California.

One group of reinforcements had their enthusiastic spirits sadly dampened when they arrived on the scene too late to use the cannon they had sledded all the way from Marysville.

In today's Susanville the Roop cabin has been preserved with the "Sagebrush War's bullets still imbedded in its aging logs (right-below).

Before the Civil War had ended, Fort Umpqua at Winchester Bay was closed by the military. Its value was questioned when the paymaster arrived a little ahead of schedule to find the post completely deserted with all personnel out hunting or fishing.

A small park at Crescent City holds markers telling of the tragic sinking of the "Brother Jonathon" (left and right above). The ship struck a low lying wash rock eleven miles from the safety of the harbor. The overloaded vessel carried 242 passengers including General George Wright and gold shipments amounting to about $365,000 destined as payment for Indian treaty obligations and Fort Vancouver's military payroll.

Only 16 passengers reached shore through the raging storm. The bodies of 60 of those who perished were washed ashore during the weeks following the wreck. The fortune carried by the "Brother Jonathon" still lies strewn along the Pacific floor near Jonathon Rock.

Within two years of the close of the Civil War nearly all of Jefferson's Indian tribes had made individual treaties and moved to the reservations prepared for them. One of the largest of these was the Hoopa Reservation of northern California (below).

Part XI
Jefferson's Chinese

The first Chinese immigrants arrived in California aboard the "Eagle" in 1848. By 1852, their numbers had increased to 18,000. Over 150,000 were under contract to the six major tongs or importing companies in 1877.

Many white miners openly resented the Orientals, who retained the ancient customs, dress and religion of their native land. Willing to work for wages often as little as 25c per day plus room and board, the patient Chinese often took over deserted claims after the whites had moved to richer claims. This precaution aided in avoiding open conflict.

Upon these workers was laid the blame for many economic problems created by the whites themselves. By means of unjust laws the Chinese immigrants in Jefferson were taxed heavily for the privilege of working by both Oregon and California.

Architecture similar to that of their homeland was incorporated in the structures taken over by the Chinese in both Yreka, California (above) and Jacksonville, Oregon, (below).

Living sometimes only on tea, rice and skunk cabbage, the Chinese miner (left-above) who struck a rich claim was easily identified because of his extravagant purchases of the favorite luxuries, which included chicken, pig, cocoanut, hard candy and gin.

At Weaverville, the Joss House (right-above), now a California state monument, provides today's viewer with a never to be forgotten visit into the past. The three ancient altars (left-below), tapestries mounted with tiny mirrored glass (right-below) and the tables where the prayer rituals were performed remain intact with the furnace which has burned the offerings of countless Chinese.

A Weaverville gully, known as Five Cent Gulch, was the scene of the 1854 "Chinese War" between the four tongs working in Trinity County, California. The feud apparently developed from a gambling debt between the Yong-wa company men from Hong Kong and three other tongs called the Canton men.

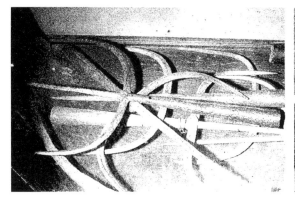

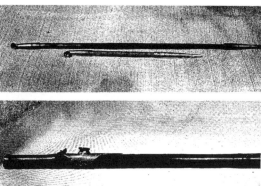

In Weaverville's Courthouse Museum are weapons forged by local blacksmiths for the battle (left-above). These 3 tined forks were attached to wooden handles between 6 and 8 feet long.

On the day of the battle nearly every miner in Trinity County was on hand to watch the proceedings and lay bets on which company would win. One white miner decided to get the fight started with a bang and fired his pistol into the assembled crowds of Chinese. This same gentleman also holds the honor of having been the only recorded white casualty.

Since the Orientals were not permitted to own firearms there were only a few killed in the Chinese War.

The Yong-wa tong drove the Canton men from the field of battle. As the field cleared two contestants continued fighting for about 15 minutes, each calmly stabbing the other with the crude iron forks until one fell dead. The survivor also joined his celestial ancestors within 2 weeks.

Among the Chinese articles displayed in Jefferson's museums are a wide variety of pipes used for tobacco and opium (right-above). Though many of these people never used opium the belief universally accepted in the mining regions was that all Orientals were addicted to the drug (below).

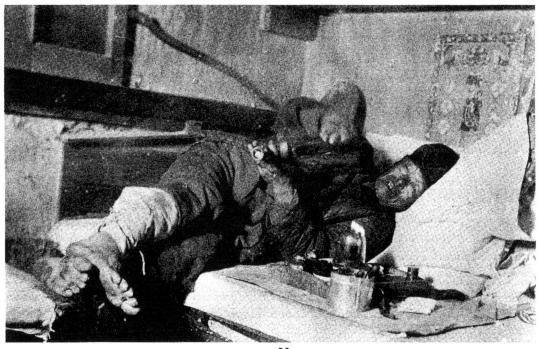

The portable weighing scales could be used by the Chinese to measure either opium or gold (left-above).

These people left their mark on Jefferson's landscape. Century old stone walls, ditches and wells built by these patient workers are still providing service today.

Because the bones of the deceased were returned to their native China in earthern jars or coal oil cans, few Chinese graves remain in Jefferson. Crude headstones (right-above) were used to mark the grave until the bodies were removed for shipment home.

For this temporary interment, the Chinese buried their own with all of the pomp and colorful ceremony peculiar to their homeland (left-below).

During the months that followed a funeral, the custom of covering the grave with offerings of coins, food and candy served to delight many of Jefferson's white small fry. These youngsters frequently returned home from a visitation to Chinese burial grounds with completely indifferent appetites.

With the completion of the transcontinental railroad and the failure of the Bank of California, the Oriental population was made the scapegoat for every white failing to produce a stable economy. Looting, pillaging and even lynching by ruthless white gangs throughout the 1870's (right-below) was condoned by the general public throughout both Oregon and California.

In 1892, Lindsay Applegate initiated an appeal for the establishment of a new Southern Oregon military post to take the place of Fort Lane, abandoned in 1857.

Ashland and Yreka wanted such a post built at Tule Lake where it could serve as a protective agency against the Modoc tribes, while Jacksonville wanted the location to be closer to that community so their merchants could participate in the trade benefits. The Klamath Lake site was chosen after a topographical survey party under Lt. Col. Drew had examined much of southeastern Oregon. The first Fort Klamath, a log blockhouse, was built in 1863.

The later fort (below) was erected at a point between Klamath and Goose lakes, near the southern emigrant road and about six miles above the later established Klamath Indian Agency.

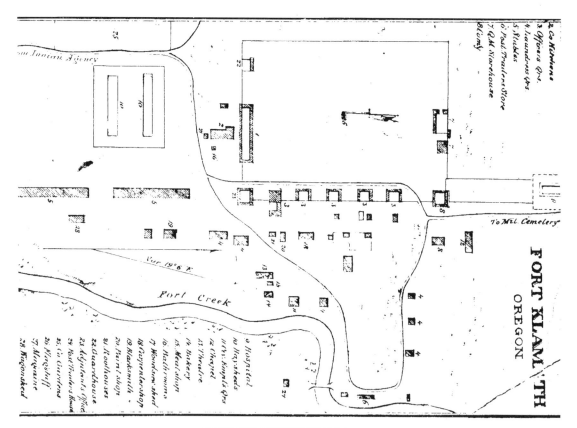

FORT KLAMATH
OREGON

This same year a George Nurse took up his land claim on which began a community named Linkville because of its location on the Link River, outlet of upper Klamath Lake (above). This name was later changed to Klamath Falls because of a low falls on the river now covered by a power dam.

A treaty drawn with the Modocs placed that tribe within bounds of the territory of their traditional enemies, the Klamath. Only the untiring efforts of Lindsay Applegate, who assumed the duties of agent for the Klamath Reservation, prevented the Indians from becoming too dissatisfied with their poor bargain.

Capt. O. C. Knapp who replaced Applegate in 1869 as agent, was a proponent of the old army school standards of "spit and polish" and "on the double." This philosophy conflicted drastically with the leisurely mode of normal Indian life.

After suffering the indignity of moving their encampment twice to prevent theft of their property by the Klamath Indians along with the curses of Knapp for bothering the agent with their problems, a group of Modocs under Kientapoos, a sub-chief, left the reservation and returned to their old home on Lost River.

A company of soldiers sent to bring the warriors back to the reservation were routed and after a raid on the adjacent ranches, the Modocs entrenched themselves in an almost impregnable position in the caves of the Lava Beds near the Oregon - California border (above).

In January, 1873, a combined white force of 400 men attacked the small band of not more that 53 Modocs and lost more than 39 dead in their first assault.

Reporting techniques developed by the news press during the Civil War were used here for the first time in covering an Indian war. The photographs recording the scene for official government records were able to note the latest in field ambulances (left-below); the rugged terrain of the area (center-below), and the army encampment south of Tule Lake (right-below).

THE LAST STRONGHOLD—DISMOUNTED CAVALRY OCCUPYING THE LAVA BEDS—[FROM A SKETCH BY J. M. WELLS.]

For a period of five and one half months, this handful of warriors inflicted heavy casualties among the more than 1,200 soldiers and volunteers who encircled them (above).

The army set up a permanent camp to begin peace negotiations with the Modocs. The treaty commission met on Good Friday in 1873 despite the warnings of Winema, wife of the interpreter, Jeff Riddle. The group, led by General Elward Canby, Commander of the Dept. of Columbia, was suddenly attacked near the tent (left-below) set up for use in the event of rain during the scheduled talks. Canby and a Methodist minister, the Reverend Eleazar Thomas, were killed by Kientapoos and Boston Charley.

A cross (center-below) was erected on the spot where Canby fell. His body was taken to Portland, Oregon, for a funeral held at the Washington Guard Armory (right-below).

How long the Modocs could have continued their resistance (left-above) will never be known. Their short supply of water, melted from ice in the caves after the army had captured the few hundred yards of ground between the stronghold and the lake's edge, finally forced the warriors to move from their position.

The continuing blunders of the military (center-above) continued to cost many white lives.

With the help of the Warm Springs Reservation Indian allies the army finally managed to force the Modocs to surrender.

Even after the war had ended and the Modoc leader Kientapoos (called "Captain Jack" by the whites), had been captured, innocent members of the tribe being transported under military protection were fired upon by volunteers and several killed. Some of the residents of Yreka who sympathized with the Modoc cause were hanged in effigy by the vengeance seeking whites during the course of the trials held at Fort Klamath (right-above).

On October 3, 1873, Capt. Jack, Schonchin John, Black Jim, and Boston Charley were hanged and buried near the enlisted men's barracks (below).

During the Lava Bed war, military supplies were freighted from Yreka, over Topsy Grade (left-above) to Laird's Landing on Lower Klamath Lake (right-above). Here the freight was loaded aboard paddle wheel steamers (right) for delivery to the troops.

When peace had been restored many of the Indian reservation supplies (below) continued to flow over this route.

Some of the Klamath Lake steamers were fitted out to provide passenger service (left-above).

Wagons from Ashland (right-above) delivered goods to Klamath Falls by way of the old Applegate Trail route.

The community of Ashland began in 1852 with a water powered sawmill (left-below). During the next year a flour grist mill was erected and in 1868 the industrial efforts were expanded to include a woolen mill. Because of the manufacturing nature of its beginning, the name "Ashland Mills" (right-below) was officially carried by the post office until 1871 when it was shortened by dropping the "Mills" designation.

Part XIII
From Pack Horse to Iron Horse

The history of Jefferson's freight transportation began with the flow of seemingly endless streams of pack horses and mules over the Indian trails linking Oregon's Willamette Valley with the Sacramento of California. The backs of these animals were piled high with merchandise destined for the gold fields (left-above).

Within a single decade, freight wagons (right-above) had nearly completely replaced the packers on the principal through routes.

The freighters travelled about 50 miles per day at an average speed of 4 miles per hour. A 40 horse team could pull a freight wagon and 2 trailers hauling a 30 ton load.

Collars of the lead horses or mules were mounted with brass or copper bells to warn others traveling the curved mountain roads of the freighter's approach (left-below).

Though the freighters operated more efficiently and at costs considerably below the packers, Jefferson's merchants were soon engaged in an effort to build a railroad between Sacramento and Portland.

Even before the beginning of the Civil War, surveyors had started to seek the most suitable route to lay rails through Jefferson's rugged mountain passes (right-below).

To stimulate interest in the building of a railroad to San Francisco, the 1864 Oregon Legislature offered $250,000 to any firm to lay 100 miles of track south from Portland.

Californians from Marysville and Oregonians from Jacksonville tried unsuccessfully to begin the work, but lack of funds prevented further action.

The next attempt to begin the railroad through Jefferson was made in 1867 with one group of Portland businessmen wanting the rails laid on the east bank of the Willamette River, while another preferred service along the west bank.

The east bank builders began with much fanfare and ceremony (below). The west side activity was soon taken over by Ben Holladay, the former stagecoach king, whose pockets bulged with the proceeds from selling his holdings to Wells Fargo. Soon outdistancing the opposing company to receive official sanction as the approved Oregon railroad builder, Holladay expended his great fortune and sold about 11 million dollars worth of bonds in Germany to lay rails as far as Roseburg. This point was reached in December, 1872. Here the extravagant era of Holladay's control of the Oregon & California railroad ended.

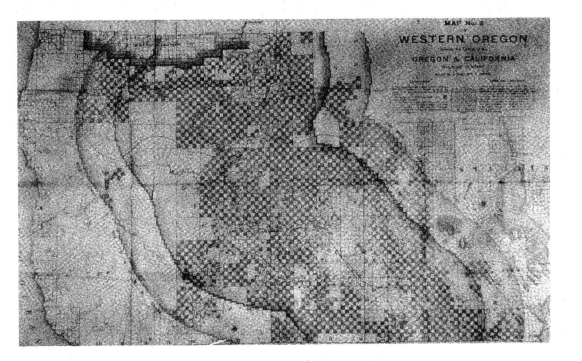

To spur the contest of the two railroads competing along the Willamette, a prize of lands grants had been added to the rewards offered the firm to first complete 20 miles of track from Portland.

These grants awarded every other section or square mile in a 40 mile wide belt along the railroad route. To compensate for those sections already occupied by settlers, the railroad builder was allowed to choose from sections in additional 20 mile strips adjoining the belt (above).

To hold the valuable grants and protect their interests, the German stockholders selected Henry Villard as Holladay's successor.

Villard's company raised many more millions in the United States and began the almost herculean task of building a railroad to the east from Portland while at the same time completing the route to California.

An attempt to move the abundant crops from Jefferson's northern Umpqua valley by an all water route was made before the railroad reached Roseburg. Steamboats were already in service in the tidewater area between Winchester Bay and Scottsburg (above). In 1870, Captain Hahn, in his 90 foot stern wheeler, the "Swan," made his way up the Umpqua River to Roseburg (below).

The thirty foot wide boat could float in water 18 inches deep. In areas where headway could not be made under power, the vessel was pulled upstream by tying the 150 foot anchor cable to an upriver tree or rock and winching the boat forward with the windless.

Roseburg residents were amazed to hear the "Swan's" whistle as she rounded the Umpqua River bend to tie up at Farquar's Island.

A plan to operate the waterway freight route between Canyonville and the coast for 7 months of the year was abandoned when the railroad from Portland reached Roseburg in 1872.

Operating from temporary camps set up along the right-of-way (left-above), the work crews, which included 4000 Chinese laborers, blasted tunnels through Jefferson's mountains (right-above) and built high trestles to span the creeks and gullies(right). The rails reached Grants Pass in December, 1883 and the first train from Portland arrived at that station Christmas Eve.

Following a nearly straight line across the Rogue valley floor from Gold Hill (left-above), the rails bypassed Jacksonville by 5 miles. Just beyond Central Point (right-above) a new station to be called "Middle Ford" was planned. The engineer in charge had come from Medford, Mass., and made a minor correction in the name to read Medford, Oregon (below).

The roadbed between Ashland and Redding required three more years to build because of the difficult bridges and fills needed in crossing the Siskiyous.

The rails had been laid to Redding, California, in 1881. The spelling of this name also caused considerable confusion on maps of that time. Although the community had been established on Pierson Reading's Mexican land grants, Rancho Bueno Venura, and its name selected in honor of that early settler, the spelling on most maps appeared the same as that of the Central Pacific Railroad land agent, B. B. Redding.

One of the principal repair yards was set up in Ashland (right). The completion of the railroad through Jefferson was celebrated with the usual golden spike ceremony being held here. The event was depicted (below) showing the spike piercing the state seals of both Oregon and California, linking them together. It heralded the end of the passengers helping to push the stage coach up every steep rise. In direct contrast, the engine (Number 87, to match the year) is speeding through the tunnelled mountains with the greatest of ease.

SUPPLEMENT TO THE WEST SHORE, PORTLAND, OREGON.

The first through train passed through Jefferson in December, 1887, (left-above). Completion of the line brought an end to the north-south stage coach traffic (right-above), though they continued to serve as feeder lines to remote inland and coastal areas until a decade beyond the turn of the century.

It took some years to establish schedules well enough to keep trains from meeting head on (left).

Jacksonville, like many communities similarly cut off from the main road, built "short lines" to retain contact with the changing world (below).

Part XIV
Culture Comes to Jefferson

Lack of the "gentle sex" presented one of the major problems in early Jefferson. Shortage of female partners made it mandatory to "elect" the dancer who was to "follow" (left-above).

The first lady "entertainers" (right-above) fairly suited the rugged mining clientele to which they catered, but it was not until after the initial boom years that most miners began to send for their wives and loved ones.

One of the first needs of the pioneer homemakers was a place of worship more appropriate than the saloons oc-

casionally used by itinerant ministers. Ingenius fund raising methods were employed by these shrewd women. In building the Jacksonville Methodist Church (left-below), a group of the very determined invaded the saloons and gaming houses. Embarassed miners "contributed" generously in their anxiety to have the ladies leave these premises not normally visited by respectable female society.

Among the many early Catholic churches still serving Jefferson's remote mining regions is one in Happy Camp (right-below).

Among the first to bring international recognition to Jefferson was Cincinatus Hiner Miller, more familiarly known as Joaquin Miller, the "Poet of the Sierras". During his 1871 visit to London to appear before the crowned heads of Europe he was hailed as "the Byron of America". Perhaps his best known poem is "Columbus".

In later years, with other "old timers" like Oliver Cromwell Applegate, Lindsay's son, he enjoyed "lie swapping" sessions (left-above).

Miller resided for brief periods in many of Jefferson's towns. Early Canyonville (right-above) made a shrine of the shack he had once occupied.

Rutherford B. Hayes toured the western seaboard with his wife "Lemonade Lucy" in 1880. The season's highlights for many of Jefferson's socially elite was the presence of this distinguished couple at the welcoming parties held in their honor. Though no liquor was served the president or his lady, their share was dutifully consumed by Civil War hero, Wm. T. Sherman, who accompanied the Hays entourage.

Between Jefferson's rail terminals at Redding and Roseburg, the journey was made by stagecoach (left-below).

Around the turn of the century the fad of "cure-all" hot mineral baths brought throngs of visitors to Ashland (right-below) and other "health resorts" of central Jefferson.

Public schools progressed from a single room, self contained unit as still stands at Golden, Oregon (left-above) to the more elaborate double seating desks in Medford (right-above).

The beautiful campus of present Southern Oregon College at Ashland had its beginning as a Methodist institution called Ashland Academy in 1869 (right). After a shaky financial start, it was designated an official state normal school in 1882.

Even in its early years, the college could point to such conveniences as "school busses" (left-below) and took pride in its active participation in the manly sport of basketball.

Pictures of early teams would indicate the athletic department's uniforms were somewhat less expensive than those used today (right-below).

Many of Jefferson's communities built opera houses to accommodate the productions of travelling companies as well as ones produced by local talent. Among these was the attractive brick structure erected in Grants Pass, Oregon (above).

The Chautauqua building in Ashland (left) offered lectures, music and drama.

In the Grants Pass town band of 1885 (left-below), principal requirement for membership was the possession of an instrument. The ability to read music was not considered mandatory.

Ashland's more professionally garbed organization occasionally boarded the train for a Sunday outing at Coles Station on the other side of the Siskiyous (right-below).

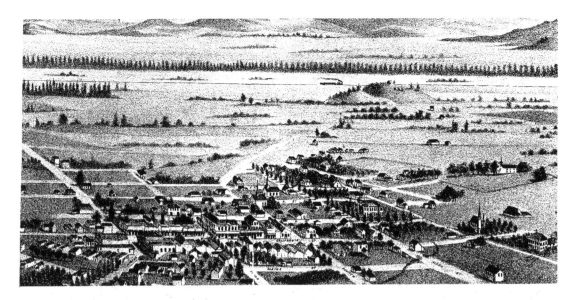

During the 1870's, Abigail Scott Duniway visited many of Jefferson's Oregon towns including Jacksonville. Her mission was to spread the gospel of equal voting rights for women. Jacksonville, one of Jefferson's major communities (above) distinguished itself by being recorded as the only "coarse mining town" to pelt this distinguished speaker with overaged eggs.

A number of the pictures contained in this volume are the product of Jacksonville's early photographer Peter Britt. Fortunately for today's historians his pictures captured many of Jefferson's early scenes to provide a photographic record of the area's cultural as well as its physical growth. Many of these pictures are displayed in a reproduction of his original studio at the Jacksonville Museum (left-below).

Outdoor darkrooms, such as Britt used in making the first pictures taken of Crater Lake (right-below), were usually set up by all frontier photographers. Distances to such scenes were too great to return home without positive proof of successfully exposed glass plates.

Part XV
Industry and the Changing Scene

Until the 1900's mining continued to hold first position as Jefferson's principal source of revenue. During the industry's first half century, production methods made a number of changes. The crushing of ore from hand hammering and rocker washing (left-above) wes succeeded by general use of the Mexican designed arrastra of mule (right-above) and water power (left). These, in turn, were outmoded by the introduction of the steam powered stamp mills (left-below). The steam age, however, did not completely eliminate all use of the earlier type horsepower (right-below).

The earliest methods of panning and placer mining (above) were replaced by the hydraulic washing method first introduced in California's Calaveras County. Using a hose leading from a high creek, the system is still in use in some parts of Jefferson today (right).

The nozzles of these "giants" ranged in lengths from 3 to more than 18 feet (left-below).

The huge dredges which float in lakes of their own making are still a part of Jefferson's landscape along the Klamath River (right-below).

When the mining industry was at its zenith, lumber prices ranged up to $250 per thousand board feet. Huge logs were hauled out of the dense forests by teams of oxen or horses (left-above). In much of Jefferson the loggers used "big wheels" (right-above) which could easily clear stumps and underbrush without the benefit of a "skidroad" (left). Some logs were delivered to the mill on wagons with wheels made from banded sections of tree trunks (left-below). Some of these methods were discontinued with the introduction of steam tractors (right-below).

Nearly all the methods previously used in midwest logging were employed to haul Jefferson's logs from the woods. These ranged from the logging railroad (above) to water lubricated flumes (right). To drop logs down to the Klamath River where they could be floated to the 1888 Klamathon mills, a 2,650 foot shute was blasted out of the mountainside (below). As logs plunged into the stream a 75 to 100 foot impact splash quenched fires ignited by the 90 mile an hour downhill trip.

The earliest of Jefferson's sawmills were of the two man whipsaw type (above). Operators could produce one to two hundred board feet of planks per day. Water powered sawmills fed from small dams (left) replaced the whipsaw and finished lumber was delivered to remote mining areas by mule pack train (below).

Lumber was also loaded on schooners by chutes for delivery to the major Pacific ports (left-above).

Because of the abundant timber supply along Jefferson's Pacific shore, many coastal towns entered the business of shipbuilding. The "Western Shore" (right), built at North Bend in 1874 earned international fame as the fastest windjammer of her time. She made the passage from Oregon to Liverpool in 97 days.

The first shipyard of this region was established in 1855 at Coos Bay (below) which was then called Marshfield.

Jefferson's fishing industry began with the packing of salted salmon on the Sacramento River. The first fish cannery began operation at the mouth of Rogue River during the 1890's (left-above).

A going price of $1.10 per pound for flour encouraged the farming of many acres (right-above) and the rich harvests called for the building of many gristmills whose grinding stones had to be brought around the Horn (left-below).

By 1889 Medford, Oregon had established itself in the fruit industry with imported pear seedlings (right-below).

The turn of the century found Jefferson's geographically isolated region beginning to reveal its great potential. Raw materials from the great forests, rich farms and prolific orchards were being exported to every corner of the world. Industries to process the bountiful harvests were born, and the area's natural beauty began to draw visitors from all sections of the nation.

The determined efforts expended over the last century plus would indicate Jefferson's citizens to be well aware of the geographic and economic similiarities that bind their individual destinies.

Between the mid 1800 and 1941 State of Jefferson movements, several lesser moves toward state secession were made.

When the 1877-78 California legislature decided to revise its state constitution, a "State of Shasta" was once again seriously considered. After this had failed, no further agitation was evidenced until the southeastern counties of Oregon began a "State of Siskiyou" in 1909. This movement was soon joined by the regular southern Oregon and northern California rebels. Though wholeheartedly supported by such news dailys as the Medford Mail Tribune,

this attempt too, fell by the wayside in 1910.

Though these many separate statehood efforts have not proven successful the State of Jefferson will continue to play a role distinctly different from the remaining areas of California and Oregon. Knowing no exact boundaries, Jefferson will remain a state of Nature's own division — geographically, topographically and emotionally. In many ways it is a domain unto itself — self-sufficient, with water, fish and wildlife, farm and orchard land, forest and mineral resources to exist on its own.

In today's changing world, with its varied and complex new fields of endeavor, our mythical "State of Jefferson" has become that final remaining link between ages-old serenity of nature's bountiful forests and the new technological age of advanced sciences.

The Josephine County Historical Society and the author wish to acknowledge their debt and sincere gratitude to the many kind people whose pictures and objects of historical interest have made this publication possible. It is our sincere wish that the name of each person whose unselfish contribution of personal time and effort could have been written here. We wish also to thank the following organizations for their courteous assistance:

The Bancroft Library
The California Historical Society
California State Indian Museum
Coos-Curry County Historical Society
Douglas County Historical Society
Fort Jones Museum
The Grants Pass Daily Courier
Humbolt County Historical Society
Oregon Historical Society
The Oregonian
Oregon State Highway Commission

Oregon State Archives
The Sacramento Bee
The San Francisco Chronicle
San Francisco Maritime Museum
Siskiyou County Historical Society
Southern Oregon Historical Society
Trinity County Historical Society
U.S. National Archives
U.S. Office of Indian Affairs
University of Oregon Library
Wells Fargo History Room

ABOUT THE AUTHOR

Jack Sutton was born January 18, 1915, in Oakland, California. He received his B. S. and Master's degrees in education from Southern Oregon College, Ashland, Oregon. During the past 15 years he has conducted classes in United States and regional history for graduate and undergraduate college courses. Through this same period he also served as a full time classroom teacher for secondary public schools in Lincoln, Josephine and Jackson counties of Oregon.

Before entering the field of education on a full time basis in 1949, Mr. Sutton's background included work in aeronautical engineering, supervisory personnel training for the War Production Board and the coordination of trade and industry programs for the Oregon State Department of Vocational Education.

The author of many articles and several books concerning the Pacific Northwest, Mr. Sutton is considered one of the foremost authorities on the history of Southern Oregon and Northern California. A more detailed biography of Mr. Sutton is carried in the 1965 edition of Marquis' "Who's Who in the West."

—Josephine County Historical Society

Made in the USA
Charleston, SC
10 August 2013